More than a Chatbot

Mascha Kurpicz-Briki

More than a Chatbot

Language Models Demystified

 Springer

Mascha Kurpicz-Briki
Applied Machine Intelligence
Bern University of Applied Sciences
Biel/Bienne, Switzerland

ISBN 978-3-031-37689-4   ISBN 978-3-031-37690-0   (eBook)
https://doi.org/10.1007/978-3-031-37690-0

Cover Illustration: © metamorworks/stock.adobe.com

This Springer imprint is published by the registered company Springer Nature Switzerland AG
The registered company address is: Gewerbestrasse 11, 6330 Cham, Switzerland

Paper in this product is recyclable.

Acknowledgments

I would like to thank my interdisciplinary project partners who inspired me to write this book, including especially the Horizon Europe project "BIAS: Mitigating Diversity Biases of AI in the Labor Market", and my research group and other research colleagues for the inspiring discussions and suggestions on the topic of this book.

In particular, I would like to thank the reviewers for their helpful comments, ideas, and suggestions on the book proposal and the manuscript: Souhir Ben Souissi, Sarah Dégallier Rochat, Ralf Kurpicz, Martin Spätig, Roger A. Søraa, Jürgen Vogel, and three anonymous reviewers. A special thanks goes to Alexandre R. Puttick for the extensive discussions and detailed reviews throughout this project. Big thanks also to Ralf Gerstner and the team from Springer for supporting me throughout the process.

Finally, I would like to thank my family for their continuous support and inspiring discussions and suggestions, empowering me to write this book.

Contents

About the Author

Mascha Kurpicz-Briki is professor for data engineering at the Bern University of Applied Sciences in Biel, Switzerland, and co-leader of the research group Applied Machine Intelligence. In her research, she is investigating how to apply digital technology, in particular machine learning and natural language processing (NLP), to social and community challenges. This includes applications for healthcare, as well as research in the field of fairness in NLP, where she investigates how to measure and mitigate bias in word embeddings and language models. In this context, she is leading the technical work package of the Horizon Europe project "BIAS: Mitigating Diversity Biases of AI in the Labor Market." She is interested in human-centered applications, following the principle of augmented intelligence – supporting humans instead of replacing them.

1

Introduction

Welcome to the Future

The latest achievements in the field of *artificial intelligence* (AI) pose many challenges to society. For the broad public, including researchers and professionals from domains outside of AI, the border between what is the technically possible and science fiction is getting blurrier.

The term artificial intelligence is a rather generic term. It has many inequivalent interpretations, and the conflation of these leads to exaggerated expectations and assumptions about how AI technology works.

The main approach behind the technologies referred to as artificial intelligence nowadays is *machine learning* (ML). Machine learning enables a computer to learn from examples for the purpose of solving tasks on similar data that it has not seen before. Although the foundations of machine learning date back to the 1960s, high computational and data demands relegated it to more of a side curiosity in the field of computer science for several decades. This changed in the new millennium, as the power of computer hardware and the advent of big data (the examples the computer learns from) culminated to the point that ML began to achieve impressive results. Machine learning can be applied in different fields, and the examples from which the computer learns can be of different data types, such as images, texts, videos, or a conventional data table.

The field of *natural language processing (NLP)* investigates interactions between computers and human language, including the development of methods for the automatic analysis or generation of text. Different methods have been employed in the past to achieve this, and nowadays, this sort of processing benefits leans heavily on advances in machine learning. The meeting of machine learning and NLP has given rise to language models, as illustrated in Fig. 1.1. These are statistical models that aim to describe patterns in written language and can be used, among other things, for text generation. Language models are what's behind the curtain in some of the latest hyped products, including ChatGPT.

Chatbots in the Media

The topic of artificial intelligence has been ubiquitous in the broad media over the last few years. In particular, *generative AI* received a great deal of attention (and some notoriety) as an example of the capacity for machine learning-based software to generate (fake) images. Language models (which can be seen as generative AI for text) have only recently been covered in more detail since late 2022 with the release of ChatGPT by OpenAI.

ChatGPT is a conversational chatbot that provides human-like answers to user-written prompts and can do so in several languages. Its responses can seem sound and eloquent and are superficially very plausible, but upon closer inspection, it turns out that the answers can contain incorrect or misleading information. For example, it is known to create references to imaginary law texts or books.

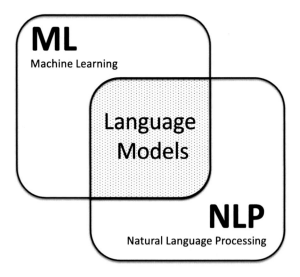

Fig. 1.1 Language models in the context of machine learning (ML) and natural language processing (NLP)

Whereas from an expert technical perspective, at the point of release in late 2022, the capabilities of ChatGPT seemed impressive, yet not surprising, the broad public was impressed – and frightened. Reactions ranged from sensing real emotions and consciousness in the answers of ChatGPT to fear of job loss and students cheating on exams. Perhaps it was because this was the first time that a language model was made easily accessible to the general public?

AI and the General Public

Contemporary history is being written in the context of digital transformation. To take an active role in this process, the broad public needs to be included in the discourse and steer, along with politicians, scientists, engineers, and practitioners, the digital society of the future toward the responsible and reasonable use of new technologies in the field of artificial intelligence. To be able to participate in this discussion, the public needs to understand the technical basics underlying these technologies. Only such an understanding allows a measured assessment of what is realistically possible with them, what are the limitations, and what is only science fiction. That is why I decided to write this book. As a data engineer and researcher in applied machine intelligence with a technical background in computer science, I am interested in how the responsible use of AI technology can be achieved. This requires dialogue with the general public. In this book, I want to give the non-technical reader a better understanding of how language models (such as the one ChatGPT is based upon) work, their amazing capabilities, and their limitations.

Who Is This Book For?

Whereas these technologies are becoming omnipresent in research, work environments, and society, the general public still has too little literacy regarding them. In the interdisciplinary research projects on which I have collaborated as a technical partner, a basic understanding of the technical concepts for the non-technical project partners has proven to be essential. Achieving such an understanding can be time-consuming and sometimes difficult, as different working cultures meet and communicate. However, I have experienced a great appreciation for technical explanations of new technologies in non-technical language. The fact that my project partners found my explanations valuable inspired me to write this book.

I have written this book to provide the broad public the necessary background information about text analysis and text generation to be able to sensibly participate in the public discourse of how and under which conditions the use of AI technologies is acceptable. This technology has the potential to radically affect our life, work, and education in the long term. For example, essays, articles, and advertisement slogans can all be generated and customized for a specific target audience. Translating technical concepts into visual slides and comprehensive explanations for my computer science students is already challenging, and explaining these contents for a broad public is even more so. Yet, it is of the utmost importance in today's world to make accessible explanations available, and I see it as our task as technical researchers to do so.

In this book, I will dive into some quite technical topics in the different chapters. The book is aimed for a general audience, explaining mathematical or technical background as necessary. Therefore, the book will of course not be able to fully cover the entirety of either machine learning or natural language processing. I will however refer to more technical computer science textbooks and literature that may be of interest to some readers.

Last but not least, I will provide you with a better understanding of what the work of data engineers[1] actually looks like. For people from other fields, it is often hard to imagine what the tasks and subjects a data engineer deals with actually are.

This book targets in particular the following, non-exhaustive list of readers:

- Non-technical readers from the broad public interested in learning more about AI and, in particular, language models
- Researchers from other domains such as medicine, social sciences, humanities, or economics interested in applying AI technologies
- Technical students new to machine learning and natural language processing, looking for a general soft introduction

After having read this book, I want you to be confident in participating in public discussions about how this new generation of language models will impact society. You will be aware of the risks and pitfalls these technologies can bring along and how to deal responsibly when making use of tools built from AI technology in general. I want you to have the necessary basic understanding of the technology to enable the discussion of AI and its social repercussions, at least at a high level, with technical people, thus opening the

---

[1] I am using the term data engineer here in broad sense, including different engineers ranging from software developers, machine learning specialists, to data scientists.

technical development of AI technologies to the particular thoughts, needs, and expertise of the people it will most affect.

Chapter Overview

In Chap. 2, I will introduce the concept of machine learning. Often, yet not always, when we talk about artificial intelligence, we are really talking about methods from machine learning. This is especially the case with recent breakthroughs in the field of natural language processing: the language models that we will discuss in later chapters. This introduction to machine learning will therefore give you the foundations. I will explain the different subdomains of machine learning, as well as how it differs from traditional software.

Then, in Chap. 3, I will dive deeper into the topic of natural language processing. Written language can express much more than the content of the words included in a sentence. Different methods have been developed to process written language or generate humanlike texts. This chapter gives an overview of these methodologies and indicates use cases that benefit from these technologies. You will also go one step further in your machine learning knowledge. Example by example, you will get a closer look at how the learning process actually happens, and I will introduce the concepts of neural networks and deep learning. Finally, this foundation will support the introduction of the concept of word embeddings, which allows computers (which prefer numbers over words) to process words from human languages.

In Chap. 4, I will go from word embeddings to the state-of-the-art language models that build the foundation for the latest technological advances, including the societal questions their existence brings forth. As language models get more sophisticated, they create the illusion of a system with true humanlike understanding. Do they really have a sentient, conscious thought process? In the public discussion around ChatGPT, this is a regular question. I will therefore explore in detail the inner workings of transformer-based language models and expose how they are much more related to statistical probabilities than humanlike emotions. Furthermore, I will discuss the human side of the conversation. I will explain, for example, why humans respond differently to the answers provided by a chatbot than to a list of results from a search engine.

Chapter 5 covers the point that whereas the texts generated by novel text generation technologies do mostly look plausible at first glance, they might contain misinformation. This chapter discusses why this happens and how it is not necessarily the primary aim of text generation technology to be fully correct in the content it produces. Connecting to the technical descriptions from Chaps. 3 and 4, this chapter illustrates how such misinformation, for example, in the form of hallucinations, is generated, how difficult it is to technically address the problem, and the challenges that arise from this. Additionally, a short introduction to the history of chatbots is provided, and you will learn some common performance metrics used to assess machine learning models.

In Chap. 6, I will describe how societal stereotypes are encoded into language models. Connecting to the technical explanations of word embeddings from Chap. 3 and the transformer-based models in Chap. 4 and using concrete examples, this chapter introduces you to the problem of bias in natural language processing. It is furthermore discussed how this bias encoded in the language model can lead to the generation of discriminatory recommendations and texts. Finally, we will look at other limitations and risks of large language models such as the use case and ecological aspects.

Finally, in Chap. 7, I will further discuss the societal consequences of all of this. The rise of AI technologies suggests many questions regarding the collaboration of humans and smart technologies in the future, with the potential to impact the way we learn, teach, and work. In particular, the focus of this chapter lies on the future need for collaboration between humans and bots powered by language models. Given the limitations discussed in the other chapters, I will introduce the concept of augmented intelligence, empowering humans rather than replacing them. This changes the way some jobs will be executed but enables human control over potentially biased or false outcomes of applications based on language models. I will argue that, rather than fully excluding AI technology, we must integrate it in our working and learning environments in a responsible way.

2

An Introduction to Machine Learning

Overview

Whereas historically different methods were used to build AI systems, nowadays the term artificial intelligence has become almost synonymous with *machine learning*. In this chapter, we will dive deeper into this topic and understand better how and in what sense machines are capable of learning. To do so, we will introduce some analogies and terminology that will follow us throughout the book when looking at technical aspects of the text processing technologies we will eventually discuss.

We begin with the key differences between traditional computer programming and machine learning. Next, we will look at the different subdomains of machine learning, namely, supervised, unsupervised, and reinforcement learning.

Traditional Computer Programming and Machine Learning

To start, let us discuss how *machine learning* makes AI technology different from other software. In general, when producing software, programmers generate *code* in a *programming language* (a set of keywords that can be translated to machine readable format and thus easily be processed and understood by the computer).[1] Traditionally, this includes a set of instructions, being

---

[1] The focus of this book is artificial intelligence and natural language processing, so we will only look at some basic concepts of computer programming. If you are interested into some more details, and what computers can do and what not, check out (Broussard 2018).

executed one after the other, leading to a specific result. Let's look at the following example borrowed from human life rather than software:

Take 10 strawberries, 1 apple and 1 banana

Cut the strawberry into small pieces and add them in a bowl

Cut the apple into slices and add them to the bowl

Peal the banana, cut it into small pieces and add it to the bowl as well

Add 1 spoon of sugar and 3 spoons of lemon juice to the bowl

Mix all the ingredients

Put the bowl in the fridge for at least 30 minutes

If all goes well and instructions are followed, at each execution, the same result – a tasty fruit salad – will be produced. This is similar to a traditional software program. A set of instructions – often referred to as an *algorithm* – is implemented in a programming language. In such software, we have specific *input data* (in our case, the strawberries, the apples, the lemon juice, etc.) and an *output* being produced (the fruit salad).

Machine learning on the other hand works differently. Based on given data (e.g., the ingredients of our fruit salad), the machine learns or detects patterns. This is what we call the *training data* of our machine learning procedure. Simplified, the question in a traditional algorithm is "How do you proceed step-by-step to obtain a fruit salad from the ingredients?", whereas with machine learning, we ask "What can you do with or figure out about the ingredients?" For the first question, we would get fruit salad. In the case of machine learning, the result is more open. If, in the case of machine learning, we would like to obtain a fruit salad, we would show the machine the ingredients and the finished product, but, crucially, not the steps that lead from one to the other. After seeing many examples of ingredients and fruit salad, the machine learning procedure constructs its own set of rules for obtaining a fruit salad. We do not have control over how the machine eventually completes the task.

Supervised Machine Learning

Let's first take a look at supervised learning by staying in our metaphorical kitchen, where we want to train a supervised machine learning program to differentiate between pictures of raspberries and strawberries. To select whether a picture contains a raspberry or a strawberry is a so-called classification task. We provide the system several examples (and yes, usually we need *many* such examples, depending on the application we talk about thousands to millions of examples) of pictures of both strawberries and raspberries. Along with each picture, we provide a text saying whether this is a strawberry or a raspberry. This is the *right solution* of the classification task, and based on that, the machine can learn how the two berries look and, more importantly, how they can be differentiated. The result of this training is a *model*. The model is a software component that is able to classify a new image (that was not part of the training data), determining whether it belongs to one of the classes from the training process. In our case, the model makes a prediction about whether the new picture shows a strawberry or a raspberry. The careful reader might have noticed the use of the term *prediction*. A prediction is an estimation, indicating the most probable option based on the patterns recognized by the system during training. Whereas the proposed result is the most probable option according to the model, we have to understand that it can also be *wrong*. This is one of the key takeaways to bear in mind for the remainder of this book. Figure 2.1 illustrates the process of supervised learning based on pictures of strawberries and raspberries.

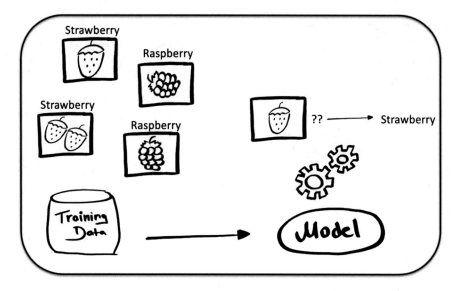

Fig. 2.1 Supervised machine learning for a classification task: Is it a strawberry or a raspberry on the picture?

Unsupervised Machine Learning

In the second type of learning strategy, unsupervised learning, we also have training data; however, we do not have *labels*. Labels are the *right solutions* we have seen in the previous paragraph, indicating whether on each picture in the training data there is a raspberry or a strawberry. This means that our training data consists of a bunch of images, some of strawberries and others of raspberries, without any indication of what is displayed on the picture. One application of unsupervised machine learning is to solve a *clustering task*. In a clustering task, the machine learning algorithm analyzes the data and tries to identify groups of similar samples. Without labels, we do not know what each of these groups contains, but we do know that the images within a single group are more similar to each other than to an image from a different group, at least according to the model. Ideally, we would have two clusters, one including all the pictures of strawberries and another one including all the pictures of raspberries. As in the previous example, the clustering might not be perfect. There might be tricky pictures of raspberries, having aspects in common with typical strawberry pictures, which are placed in the wrong group (e.g., you might be most familiar with the grocery store domesticated large strawberry, but wild strawberries are much smaller and could, to the untrained eye, be mistaken for raspberries). Figure 2.2 illustrates this example of unsupervised machine learning.

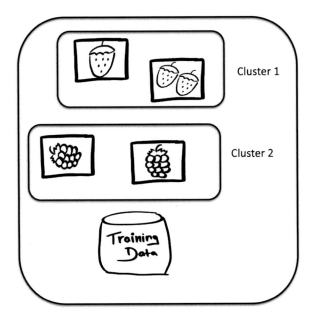

Fig. 2.2 Clustering pictures of strawberries and raspberries in groups: an unsupervised machine learning task

Reinforcement Learning

Finally, the last type of machine learning is reinforcement learning. This type of learning is similar to the supervised approach, where we gave the system information along with each image (saying, e.g., that we see a strawberry in a given picture). In the case of reinforcement learning, there is an interaction between the machine and the (possibly virtual) environment, which provides feedback during the learning process. You can imagine this as a *trial-and-error* approach.

Let's take a real-world example to illustrate this. Imagine you are asked to cut a strawberry into slices of approximately of the same size. One way to improve your skills could be by receiving feedback about the strawberry slices that have already been cut. For example, somebody next to you could say, "This slice is quite large compared to the others!" With this feedback, you would adapt your cutting method for the upcoming slices. Step by step, the results would get better. At some point, the results would be good enough to stop the training process. This process is illustrated in Fig. 2.3.

Similarly, it is possible to provide such external feedback in machine learning. Specific results can be rewarded, and thus this behavior will be reinforced in the final model. A crucial factor in reinforcement learning is how we give

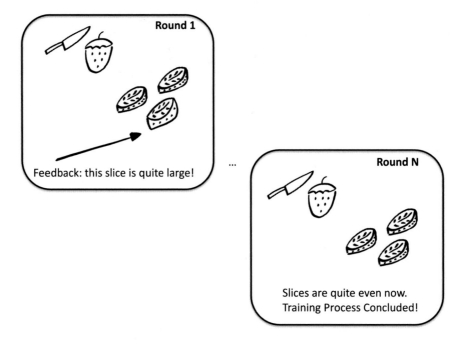

Fig. 2.3 Reinforcement learning: improvement through feedback

feedback to the machine. For instance, if the feedback doesn't take into account the number of slices, you could exploit the lack of specificity and simply not slice the strawberry at all, resulting in a trivially perfectly even slice and a pat on the back from your supervisor.

Algorithms and Artificial Intelligence

So where is the artificial intelligence (AI) here? There are a few things to clarify. In the media, often, the term *algorithm* is used in the context of AI. I want to give you some context here about this word and how its origin is slightly different from the way it is currently used in the context of AI. Generally, the word *algorithm* (derived from the name of a ninth-century Persian mathematician M. al-Khwarizmi) means a set of instructions to achieve a particular goal, for example, as we have seen previously, how to prepare a fruit salad based on a list of ingredients. An algorithm could also be a set of data processing steps we want to communicate to a computer. In traditional software, this processing is like a recipe. For example, to find the first appearance of the letter "a" in a word, we could use the following algorithm:

Input: word written in English

Steps to proceed:

Read the first letter: is it "a"? Then result is 1.

If not, read the second letter: is it "a"? Then result is 2.

etc.

Output: Position of the first appearance of "a" in the input word.

In the context of contemporary AI, the word algorithm is used to refer to the software as a whole. For example, personalized recommendations for music or movies are generally considered to be machine learning-based algorithms.

Technically, when talking about AI or machine learning and using this wording, there are actually two separate algorithms at play. For the scope of this example (and most future examples), we will consider a supervised learning setting, where the model is trained on labeled training data. To illustrate this, I want to borrow the definition from Katharina Zweig, who defines machine learning as "Automated learning by way of examples, in which decision rules are searched for [and] then stored in a statistical model" (Zweig 2022, p. 95). On one side, we have the algorithm that was used to train the model based on the training data, the process by which "decision rules are searched for." We refer to this process as the *training phase*, depicted in Fig. 2.4. The input of this training algorithm is the training data and an untrained

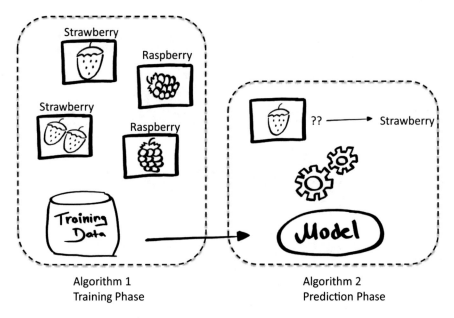

Fig. 2.4 In the training phase, the machine learning model is trained using the training data. This is where the actual machine learning happens. The resulting model is then applied in the prediction phase to new data

model, for example, one that guesses randomly. The output is a trained model. This is where the actual machine learning happens.

On the other hand, we have the statistical or *trained* model, which is the outcome of the training process and itself an algorithm that takes as input one instance of data and provides as output a prediction, based on the rules learned during the training phase. This is the *prediction phase*, where the trained machine learning model is applied to new data, typically after being deployed in whatever production setting the model was being trained for. For example, we may take as input a new picture, distinct from those in the training data, and ask whether it depicts a strawberry or a raspberry. We feed the photo to the model and receive as output its answer to that question, as illustrated on the right in Fig. 2.4.

Text Processing Ahead!

So far, we have discussed machine learning with examples based on images. The training data consisted of pictures of strawberries or raspberries. Nevertheless, the learning strategies we have seen can be applied in the same or similar manner to data of different types, e.g., text. We will now move from images to text and explore for the remainder of this book how these machine learning technologies can be applied in natural language processing. Even though we will focus on text processing and generation, the concepts and limitations we describe also apply, to a certain extent, to models dealing with other data types, such as images, video, or multimodal systems.[2]

Summary

In this chapter, we looked at three different types of machine learning. In supervised machine learning, the training data is labeled (e.g., indicating whether or not we see a strawberry in a given picture). We examined a simple classification task, training a model to differentiate between strawberries and raspberries and making predictions on new, unseen pictures. For unsupervised machine learning, we looked at the example of clustering, and finally, we learned how reinforcement learning can be used to provide feedback during the learning process and improve the results.

In the examples, we learned that machine learning models can make mistakes. Whereas they make a prediction by proposing the option that is, according to the model, the most probable solution, this solution can easily be wrong. This is a crucial point to consider when using AI technology.

We also examined the differences between traditional algorithms and machine learning. A supervised machine learning algorithm takes data in the form of inputs and desired outputs (labels) and outputs rules for getting from one to the other, whereas a traditional algorithm consists solely of rules for getting from input to desired output.

Let's now move on and dive into the fascinating world of text processing!

---

[2] In multimodal systems, different types of data are combined, such as in the model GPT-4 released by OpenAI in 2023.

3

Processing Written Language

Overview

Human language viewed from a technical perspective has been fascinating researchers for a long time. The first application of natural language processing was in 1948 at the Birkbeck College in London and consisted of a dictionary lookup system (Hancox 1996). While 1948 may be quite recent in other domains, in computer science, this is very early. Since then, a lot has happened. Today, natural language processing technologies are used in our daily lives, sometimes explicitly (e.g., when interacting with a chatbot) and sometimes behind the scenes (e.g., when using online search).

In this chapter, we will learn more about how text is processed automatically. Natural language processing refers to the automated processing (including generation) of speech and text. In this book, we use the terms text processing and natural language processing interchangeably. We will look at some common natural language processing applications, and I am quite confident that you will recognize the one or the other in recent interactions you've had with such systems. We will then have a look at some common methods from the field of natural language processing. Then, we will deepen our machine learning knowledge and introduce and understand the advantages and disadvantages of deep learning and neural networks. Finally, we will understand how words from human language can be represented as mathematical vectors and why this is beneficial for machine learning.

© The Author(s), under exclusive license to Springer Nature Switzerland AG 2023
M. Kurpicz-Briki, *More than a Chatbot*, https://doi.org/10.1007/978-3-031-37690-0_3

Natural Language Processing Applications

Automatic processing of text can be useful in many settings. Loosely inspired by the categorization of NLP applications of Lane et al. (2019), we explore some of the use cases together to unveil the potential that lies within such applications. Many of us interact unknowingly on a day-to-day basis with these technologies.

Search Engines and Writing Suggestions

Web and document search applications rely heavily on natural language processing technologies for assessing the search query (the sentence or word that you have written in the search field) and the available documents (e.g., the existing websites on the Internet that have been collected and indexed) and to identify the best-matching results. All of this happens, usually, in a fraction of a second, and you might not be aware of the extremely efficient processing happening in the background. Furthermore, some search engines propose corrections to your search query (*Did you mean:*) or provide *autocomplete* functionality by assessing the search queries entered by the user.

Natural language processing technologies can also support us while writing text. Many text processing programs underline spelling mistakes or make suggestions, on how to adapt grammar and style. Does it sound familiar to you? Then this is another use case where you have actively interacted with natural language processing technologies similar to the ones we explore in this book.

Text Classification

Let's look at another example. Have you ever wondered how the *spam filter* in your e-mail inbox works? Text processing technologies drive the analysis of the incoming e-mails and the decision of whether they are of interest to you or spam. Some e-mail providers use more advanced filtering, providing, for instance, categories such as spam, advertisement, or social media notifications. But text processing with e-mails does not end there. A further use case could be automated ranking by priority or proposing answers to e-mails, functionalities that have recently been introduced by different providers.

But let's stay with spam detection for now. Depending on the complexity of the underlying technology used by a given software product, the mechanisms to detect spam can function differently, leading also to results of varying qualities. In the simplest case, a keyword analysis based on predefined sentences or the sender's address can be done. Of course, this might still let numerous spam e-mails into your inbox. So probably (and hopefully) no spam detection system relies solely on predefined lists. We should also bear in mind that spam creators get better and better in response to better and better filters. Automatic text generators are now able to write very believable texts that are uniquely customized for different uses. It's an arms race between improving technology used to develop very realistically looking spam e-mails and technology to detect spam, both of which using the latest machine-learning-driven advancements in natural language processing.

Sorting e-mails into different categories is an example of what we, in the field of natural language processing, call a *text classification task*. When approached using machine learning, this can be quite similar to the image classification into strawberries or raspberries that we saw in the previous chapter. Assume we have a large number of examples of spam e-mails, advertisement e-mails, social media notifications, and other e-mails. All of the examples from the four categories in our training dataset are labeled, meaning that they are assigned a *tag* that indicates which category they belong to. During the training phase, the machine then identifies the particularities that differentiate these groups of texts. Finally, the model can classify a new text sample into one of the four categories, as shown in Fig. 3.1.

Recall from the previous chapter that these predicted classes are best guesses based on probability and that the quality of the result depends on the

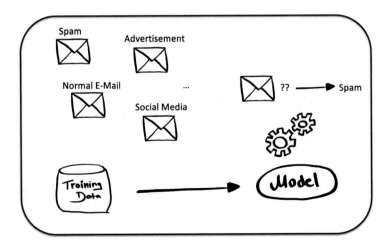

Fig. 3.1 Classification of e-mails into different categories using supervised machine learning

completeness and quality of the training data. And even in the best case, there can be mistakes. With that in mind, you will not be surprised the next time an e-mail is misclassified in your inbox.

Such text classification can also be used in other use cases. It is, for example, possible to train a machine learning model on a large number of texts from two or more different authors and thus obtain a classifier that identifies the author of a text. This kind of technology has been used to determine which parts of Shakespeare's play *Henry VIII* may have been written by somebody else, a subject that has long been debated by scholars (Plecháč 2021). Authorship attribution also plays an important role in *plagiarism detection*, software that is regularly applied in the context of scientific publishing, as well as to check student papers. Other work in the field investigates how machine learning can be used to identify hate speech or fake news on the Internet.

Sentiment Analysis

Text classification is also applied in the field of *sentiment analysis*. These methods aim to extract information from text that indicates sentiment or opinion, for example, whether a text carries a positive or negative attitude of the writer toward a product in a review text. Here again this task can be solved in different ways, starting from a very simplistic approach. If we find expressions like "poor quality," "horrible design," or "ugly interface" or, on the flipside "wonderful product," "amazing design," and "I love it," we can easily get an idea of whether the writer of the review likes or dislikes the product. However, there is an untenable multitude of ways sentiment can be expressed, and human creativity is nearly endless, so we will soon reach our limits when creating a word list of all possible positive and negative expressions. An alternative (among others) is therefore to use the methods of supervised machine learning, as we discussed for the case of the e-mail classification. Based on examples of positive texts and negative texts, a classifier is trained that is able to predict whether a new text sample is rather positive or negative. Whenever we have a problem where we want to categorize text into two or more classes, and we have sufficiently many examples available for the different classes, we can utilize this supervised learning approach.

In general, in the context of text classification tasks, we refer to *binary classification* when we have two possible groups to distinguish between, e.g., positive and negative texts and *multiclass classification* otherwise. A common example of multiclass sentiment classification could be to map review texts to their star rating from 1 to 5, as is often seen on websites where users provide feedback on, for example, movies or restaurants. We would try to use machine learning to predict the star rating (which is the label/*right answer*), based on the review texts written by the users. This would be a multiclass classification with five classes.

Text Generation

As opposed to text classification tasks, where the model takes a text as input and predicts one of the specified categories as output, other tasks take text as an input and also have text as output. We refer to these tasks as *text generation*. An example for this kind of task is *text summarization*. When dealing with hundreds of pages of text, often, the content can also be aggregated, at least at a surface level, on a few pages or even less. This task can be supported in an automated way by language models. *Chatbots* are another application of text generation. Based on texts as input, they provide text answers similar to those of a human. Chatbots can have different goals, for example, to answer customer queries and provide the information the client is looking for. Here, it is highly relevant that the information is correct. As we have seen recently with the rise of ChatGPT, the correctness of the content produced by language models and chatbots in particular is not always a given (which, naturally, might be surprising for one or the other reader). We will further explore this problem in a later chapter. For now, I want to point out that the aim of some chatbots, can also be to provide the most plausible text in terms of being as close as possible to the wording a human would choose. Other applications of text generation are the automated production of movie scripts, song lyrics, or poetry by machine learning models, and a further important use case of text generation is *machine translation*, where text is translated from one language to another, for example, from English to German. Text generation can also be the result of non-textual input, for example, when automatically generating captions for images.

Information Extraction

Another task we can conduct on texts is *information extraction*. We want to obtain structured information based on the texts, which, in contrast, is typically considered to be *unstructured data* (this applies to images too). Unstructured because the data does not have a predefined organizational principle, as opposed to, say, a table of values structured according to the row and column identities. The term *unstructured* in the context of written language is perhaps a bit confusing. When treating texts for a given language, there are of course external constraints such as the grammar of the language that might restrict up to a point the order of words or objects in sentences. However, there are still flexibilities, and not all sentences or texts have identical structure. For this reason, text is also sometimes called *semi-structured* data, which can be extended by additional information such as identifying the subject of the sentence or adding tags for the type of word (e.g., by marking *to be* as a verb).

Raw text data itself is not equivalent to data arranged in a table, with columns corresponding to say subject, verb, and object. We could extract such structured data from the text, but it's not equivalent in the sense that we can't recover the original text only from the structured table.

In the information extraction process, we want to obtain very specific data from the text. We therefore define a data structure, meaning that we describe the structured data we would like to obtain from all the different texts we plan to process. This data structure can be very different depending on the use case of the application. For example, when working with legal texts, it might be of interest to extract the paragraphs and laws mentioned in the texts. In the case of doctor's notes, we might want to extract the diagnosis from the text and ideally convert it into a standardized format, e.g., a diagnosis code.

Let's look at this in an example. The left side of Fig. 3.2 contains unstructured text. We want to extract two things from the texts (the data structure is prepared in the table on the right):

• Which types of berries are mentioned
• Whether there are persons mentioned (e.g., by using their name)

The aim of the information extraction is to provide structured information about the texts that can be further processed, either by humans or by another software component. For example, the data table generated could be easily used to quickly get all the texts where Anna is mentioned or including information about strawberries.

From Applications to Methods

The use case examples we have been going through in this section are not a complete list of all possible applications of natural language processing. The selected use cases rather aim at giving you an impression of the power of these technologies, the wide range of uses, and how they can potentially support

From unstructured text to structured data

Text 1:
The sun was shining and the weather was good. There was a large field full of strawberries, however, no raspberries were planted in this region.

Text Nr.	Berries mentioned	People mentioned
1	strawberries, raspberries	-
2	blueberries	Anna

Text 2:
Anna was very hungry, so she decided to buy some blueberries. They were very tasty and she liked them.

Fig. 3.2 Extracting structured information from unstructured texts

our daily work and life. I also want you to take away from this section that, depending on the complexity of the problem and the expected outcomes, very different technologies can be applied. This can range from simple methods to more complex methods such as deep learning and large language models. It is part of the art and craft of the data engineer to identify the right method for the given application, among the vast range of possibilities available in today's toolkits and research outcomes. In the upcoming sections, we will have a closer look at some of these technologies.

Introduction to Natural Language Processing Methods

Whereas recent developments in natural language processing heavily rely on machine learning, this is in general not necessarily the case. A simple text processing task could be to identify the appearances of berries in a text, based on a list of words provided to the program. In this case, there would be no training data or training phase, but a traditional algorithm being employed of the sort seen previously analogous to the fruit salad recipe. We would be processing the given sentence step by step, comparing each word to the words on the list. Such simple methods have some limitations, for example, we would

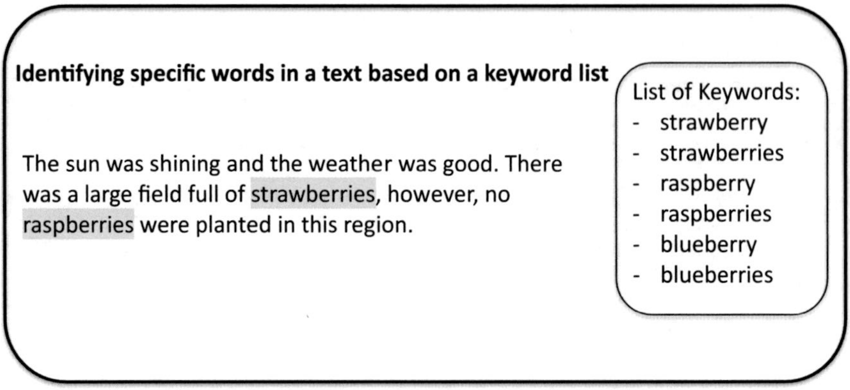

Identifying specific words in a text based on a keyword list

The sun was shining and the weather was good. There was a large field full of strawberries, however, no raspberries were planted in this region.

List of Keywords:
- strawberry
- strawberries
- raspberry
- raspberries
- blueberry
- blueberries

Fig. 3.3 Keep it simple: identifying specific words in a text based on a keyword list

have to add both the word *strawberry* and the plural form *strawberries* on the list to make sure to get them all. Figure 3.3 gives an example of such a scenario.

A priori, from the computer's point of view, the text is nothing more than a string of letters and symbols. We call the process of adding additional structure to these strings *parsing*. When looking at the text as humans, we of course see more structure – such as separated words or grammatical structure. The thing is that computers prefer dealing with numbers and doing math, and do not have, in general, the years of training that we had in order to automatically and immediately structure such texts in our heads. When parsing text, we instruct the computer to, for example, do word or sentence *tokenization*: We separate words and sentences, specifying that after each blank space, a new word starts. Or that after a period, a new sentence starts. We are instructing the computer to do so by writing our instructions in a programming language.

More advanced tagging of a text can be done by using *part-of-speech tagging*, *dependency parsing*, or *named entity recognition*.

Part-of-Speech Tagging

Part-of-speech tagging refers to the process of annotating each word with a *tag* identifying the type of word. For example, strawberry is a *noun*.

As you might imagine, these are regular tasks that need to be done over and over again in different applications. Instead of reinventing the wheel each time, the data engineer has existing software components available (so-called libraries) that can be reused as needed.

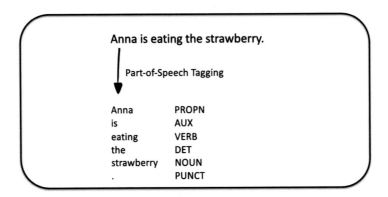

Fig. 3.4 An example of part-of-speech tagging: extracting information about the type of the words. For example, "." is considered a punctuation (PUNCT), "eating" is classified as verb, and the name "Anna" is a proper noun (PROPN)

```
nlp = spacy.load("en_core_web_sm")
doc = nlp("There was a large strawberry field.")
displacy.serve(doc, style="dep")
```

Fig. 3.5 Code snippet to visualize dependency parsing using SpaCy library

In Fig. 3.4, we see an example how this information is provided automatically by a library called SpaCy[1] that is commonly used for natural language processing.

Dependency Parsing

Let's now look at an example for dependency parsing. Dependency parsing gives us information about how the words in the sentence relate to each other. Some of us, especially the ones with a more technical background, will need to grab our grammar books when working with this kind of parsing.

To give you some intuition, we will look at a short snippet of such programming code using the programming language Python and the library SpaCy shown in Fig. 3.5.

The first line loads a model for the English language from this existing library. This would be different when processing another language. To be able to consider, for example, grammatical concepts to parse our text, we will need to have the specifics of the given language readily available. In the second line,

---

[1] https://spacy.io

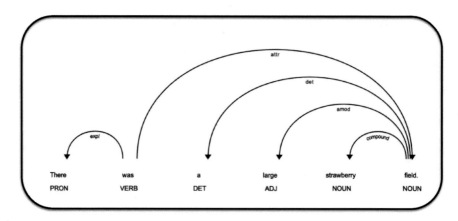

Fig. 3.6 Visualization of the dependency parsing of an example sentence using the SpaCy library

we are defining the sentence that we want to parse. The last line initiates the dependency parsing and enables a visualization. Don't worry if you do not understand the meaning of every single word in the above code snippet; the main goal is to get an understanding of how these things work.

Based on these three lines of programming code, the visualization shown in Fig. 3.6 is generated about our sentence.

We have two different kinds of information in this illustration: On one side, we can see the type of word at the bottom, which we called part-of-speech tag before (*was* is a verb, *large* is an adjective). The arrows indicate us the relations between the words in the sentence, the syntactic dependencies. For example, the words *strawberry* and *field* have been recognized as compound words. The word *large* was marked as adjectival modifier (*amod*) to the word *field* (we are not going to go too deeply into grammar at this point, but you get the idea).

Named Entity Recognition

We will now consider an example of the task of *named entity recognition*, which involves extracting relevant information from text, for example, by classifying words as organizations, geopolitical entities, or numbers.

To see this example, we use a similar code example as before, but we change the sentence and one word in the last line (replacing simply *dep* as in *dependency* with *ent* as in *entity*), as shown in Fig. 3.7.

```
nlp = spacy.load("en_core_web_sm")
doc = nlp("In 2023, thousands of strawberries were
eaten in EU countries and the US.")
displacy.serve(doc, style="ent")
```

Fig. 3.7 Code snippet to visualize named entity recognition using the SpaCy library

In 2023 **DATE** , thousands **CARDINAL** of strawberries were eaten in EU **ORG** countries and the US **GPE** .

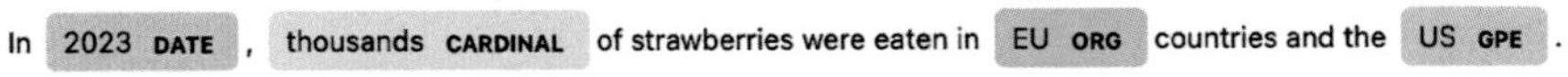

Fig. 3.8 Result of the named entity recognition example using the SpaCy library

Different named entities have been identified in our sentence, as shown in Fig. 3.8: The year 2023 has been identified as a date, the EU as an organization (ORG stands for companies, agencies, institutions), the US as geopolitical entity (GPE), and *thousands* was classified as a number (CARDINAL). There are a few more such categories (such as MONEY for monetary values), but those are among the most common ones. Automatically identifying such information in our texts can be beneficial as an entry point to more advanced text processing. We notice that in this context, the EU could be considered as a geopolitical entity rather than an organization. This serves as a reminder that such models might not work perfectly in all situations.

Inside Machine Learning

We looked at the basic procedure of machine learning in the previous chapter. The interesting question we didn't fully answer then is *how* does the learning actually happen.[2] We will first define classical machine learning and see how this is different from deep learning and neural networks. Sounds difficult? No worries, all mathematical backgrounds required to follow this part will be gently introduced as needed. So, let's go step by step.

In this section, we will concentrate on supervised machine learning. We will use the task of sentiment analysis as an example. This means that we consider a collection of texts that are positive, i.e., express the positive attitude of the author, and another collection of texts that are negative. As you might remember, *supervised* means that each text snippet is labeled with the

---

[2] We will look at some more technical concepts but, however, will in the scope of this book not go into all the details. If you want to know it all and are willing to dive deep into the technical parts, I can recommend you the textbooks (Lane et al. 2019; Hagiwara 2021) as follow-up to this book, providing an applied step-by-step description of different NLP methods.

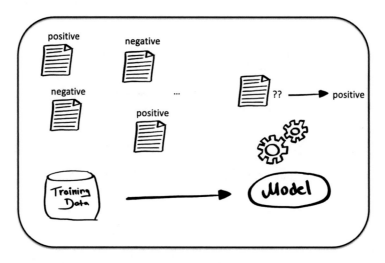

Fig. 3.9 Sentiment analysis: classifying texts as positive or negative with supervised machine learning

Table 3.1 The training data can be structured in a table, with one column for the texts and another column for the labels

Text	Label
Wow, what a cool website!	Positive
Oh no, I really think this is bad.	Negative
...	

information about whether it is positive or negative. It is a classification task, because we want to train a model that is able to classify a new, unseen text into one of the two classes, *positive* or *negative*. Figure 3.9 shows the setup of our machine learning classifier as we have seen previously for the other examples.

Now, the interesting thing here is what happens during the training phase. How is the model created, which is then able to classify the unseen texts?

Pre-processing the Training Data

The training data shown in Fig. 3.9 could be structured in a table, containing the text sample in the first row and the label in the second row, as shown in Table 3.1.

Before we can start with the training, text *pre-processing* is done. This means that we have to clean up the texts we are considering as input (i.e., the training data). In our case of sentiment analysis, these are the text samples containing positive or negative texts. We want to exclude information that is not relevant. What exactly needs to be done in this phase depends on what texts we have. For example, a typical operation is to remove additional information such as links or transforming all letters to lowercase and removing punctuation:

"Wow, this is REALLY a cool website! http://www.springernature.com"

could, for example, be adapted to the following after this phase:

"wow this is really a cool website"

We also split the sentence into single words that can be processed separately (so-called tokenization):

"wow this is really a cool website"

becomes:

["wow","this","is","really","a","cool","website"]

In some cases, we might go further and remove words that are considered insignificant for the training, so-called stop words. Lane et al. (2019, p. 51) define stop words as "common words in any language that occur with a high frequency but carry much less substantive information about the meaning of a phrase." Common stop words are, for example, *the, a,* or *on.*

Sometimes, it is also useful to use *stemming* or *lemmatization*. Both methods have the same goal: modifying words with these methods brings them in a form that allows to determine whether two words belong together, meaning that they are the same word in a different form. Stemming is a technique that identifies the word stem by cutting off parts of the word. For example, the stem of *houses* is *house*, and the stem of *runs* is *run*. However, there are some limitations with that method that it is often oversimplifying and words that we might want to differentiate are assigned to the same stem. For example, the word *meetings* is changed to *meet*, but maybe *meeting* would be the better stem (Hagiwara 2021). Also, such methods often fail with irregular words such as *caught,* where we could prefer to have *catch* instead of the stem. With lemmatization on the other hand, instead of using the word stem, the original form of the word is identified. This might seem similar to stemming but is yet different: here it is not just about cutting of parts of the word but under consideration of the language's structure, for example, for verbs, the base form before conjugation. For our examples *meetings* and *caught,* the lemmatized forms would therefore be *meeting* and *catch* respectively.

Feature Selection

We define a *feature* as a characteristic or measurable property of our data. An important and often tricky part of machine learning is *feature selection,* deciding which are the appropriate features and how important they are for training a classifier that works best on other, unseen data. Also in human decision-making, depending on the context, some aspects are more relevant than others. When making a diagnosis about a patient, the blood pressure or the description of symptoms is likely to be more relevant than the color of the T-shirt the person is wearing. Thus, the blood pressure would be a good feature for the machine learning training, whereas the color of the t-shirt would probably not be the best choice.

In the case of text processing, the feature selection could, for example, be all the words of a text. In other situations, a good feature selection might be to consider the most often occurring words, or only adjectives, depending on the use case. Let's suppose for our example that we want to do the feature selection based on the *word frequency.* We therefore need to find out which words occur the most often in our training data. More specifically, we want to find the words that are *typical* for positive texts and typical for negative texts. Some words that appear often in general might be in the top list of both groups, for example, words such as *the* or *a* (if we have removed the stop words earlier, this might be less of a problem). We can get around this by removing any words that appear in *both* the positive and the negative group. The intuition behind this is the fact that such words will not be of any use to differentiate between the two groups. Let's say we take for the sake of this example the three most frequent words of each group and end up with the following:[3]

Positive = ["good", "happy", "awesome"]
  Negative = ["ugly", "horrible", "bad"]

---

[3] Choosing the top 3 words is to keep the example simple. In a real case, we would want to choose a higher number of words.

From Words to Numbers

As mentioned earlier, computers are much better in dealing with numbers than with human language. So, what to do with those words?

Before getting deeper into this, let's look at the concept of a mathematical *vector*. In general, we are all using numbers daily. Vectors contain more information than single numbers. They consist of lists of multiple numbers, and the length of which is called the dimension of the vector. So, for example, the vector (0, -2, 5.1) is a three-dimensional vector. For a given dimension n, the collection of all possible n-dimensional vectors is an example of what's called a vector space. Vectors are typically depicted as arrows, and arrows with (a) the same length, (b) the same orientation, and (c) that are in parallel are the same vector.

In a two-dimensional vector space, vectors have two coordinates to specify their position. The first coordinate indicates their position with regard to the x-axis, and the second coordinate indicates their position with regard to the y-axis, as illustrated in Fig. 3.10. For three dimensions, we can imagine a cube with three coordinates. Starting from four dimensions (and vector spaces can have very high dimensions), it gets difficult to imagine but works analogously: in a vector space with 20 dimensions, vectors living in that space have 20 numbers composing their coordinates.

We will also need to know that between such vectors, mathematical operations such as addition or subtraction can be executed, similar to numbers.

We need to transform our words into vectors, so that the machine learning classifier can work with them. Each word will be converted into a single vector. The simplest way to do this is to use *one-hot vectors*. Each vector has dimension equal to the number of possible words in our vocabulary. In a realistic case, these can be hundreds of thousands of possible words, but let's

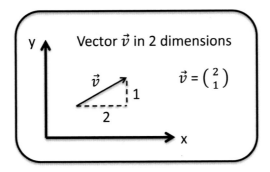

Fig. 3.10 An example of a vector with two dimensions

keep it simple and assume our language has the following vocabulary consisting of four words:

["awesome", "bad", "good", "horrible"]

The vector space (dimension) would then be 4. Therefore, each vector has four entries (two more than the example vector in Fig. 3.10). Each word would then be represented by having a vector full of *0* and having *1* only at the position of the word in the vocabulary. What do we mean by position? In the vocabulary above, the word *awesome* is at position 1, *bad* at position 2, and so on.[4] Therefore, the vector representation of *bad* would have a 1 at the position 2 and 0 for the rest of the positions:[5]

vector["bad"] = [0,1,0,0]

That's it. We have created a vector representation of our words. Clearly, this simple method provides some limitations. In four dimensions, some zeroes are forgivable, but if we have vectors of hundreds of thousands of dimensions (to cover all vocabulary of the English language), there will be many zeros that need to be stored. We will see more advanced ways to vectorize words using fewer dimensions in a later section.

Machine Learning Classifiers

After this step of *vectorization*, we have a list of vectors that are typical for positive texts and another list of vectors that are typical for negative texts. We are thus ready to train our machine learning classifier. The first thing to do is to choose the type of classifier we want to use. Different mathematical models exist, and we chose one of them depending on the data and our needs. It is also often the case that the best performing classifier cannot be predicted easily in advance. Thus, sometimes, it is very beneficial to try out different ones to find the right one for a given dataset or problem.

One such machine learning classifier is called a *logistic regression classifier*. This type of classifier is a type of *discriminative classifier* (Jurafsky and Martin 2023), which aims to learn to distinguish between two groups based on

---

[4] In computer science, we often start counting with 0 and not 1 in such situations. But it takes some time to get used to this, so let's start counting with 1 here.

[5] In the example above, the numbers inside the vector were represented one above the other, and here they are represented on the same line. This is just to improve the readability and has no specific meaning.

statistical differences. It is assessed how important the different features are to differentiate between the two groups. This happens by assigning weights, which means assigning each feature a value, measuring how important it is for the outcome. This means that it tries to figure out which are the most relevant among the words we have provided as input. This happens by looking at all the features we have provided one by one and adapting the *weights* as necessary.

To better understand what we mean by weights, let's consider the following example. We consider a strawberry plant full of wonderful, tasty strawberries in different sizes. There are some fruits, so that the plant tends to bend toward the right side. We want to study what causes the strawberry plant to bend itself. Probably, the huge strawberry contributes more to this than the tiny strawberry. Thus, the huge strawberry has a bigger weight than the tiny strawberry, as shown in Fig. 3.11.

This is similar to the weights of our features. In the beginning of the learning procedure, all words might have an equal weight. Over time, the model learns that the word *good* indicates positive and therefore gives the word *good* more weight in the positive category. Thus, after training, the model's decisions will *bend more* in the direction of positive when the word *good* is present, similar as strawberries with larger weights that have major impact on the strawberry plant bending to the right.

The Loss Function

Let's come back to the example of cutting strawberries in even slices that we have seen in an earlier chapter. With each iteration, we are getting a bit better. But how do we measure our improvement? Let's say that the desired slice size is 4 mm. We want all the slices we cut to be as close as possible to this

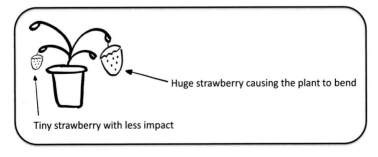

Huge strawberry causing the plant to bend

Tiny strawberry with less impact

Fig. 3.11 The huge strawberry is causing the plant to bend; the tiny strawberry has less impact

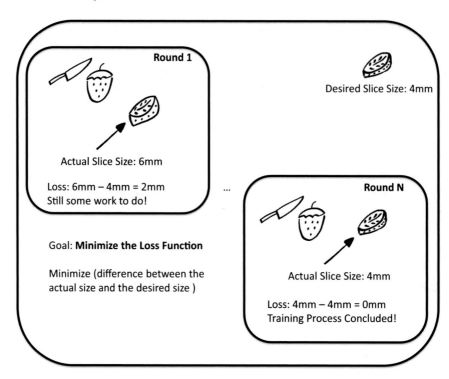

Fig. 3.12 To train the model, we need to minimize the loss. The closer we get to the desired slice size, the lower the loss gets

reference value, and we thus want to become good at cutting strawberries into slices of this specific size. Each time we cut a slice, we can compare its size to the desired slice size. We are 2 mm too large? Let's try to cut it smaller. This procedure is shown in Fig. 3.12. We improve our method, to get as close as possible to the desired strawberry slice size. In mathematical terms, we want to reduce the difference of the actual slice size and the desired slice size. In this case, we are talking about slice size, but in general terms in machine learning, we talk about the *loss function*. The aim of the learning process is to minimize this loss function. In Fig. 3.12, the loss in the beginning at round 1 is 2 mm and 0 mm in round N. The closer the loss gets to zero, the better the performance of the machine learning model. During the learning, the values of the machine learning model (such as weights) are adapted in order to minimize this loss.

An important point about the loss function is that it explicitly defines what we are *training the model* to do. The entire aim of the training is to modify the model in order to minimize the loss. This is what we mean by *learning*.

Let's now return from cutting strawberries into slices to our previous task of sentiment analysis. We want to classify a text being either positive or negative. Depending on the classifier we choose to train (e.g., the logistic regression mentioned earlier), the loss function is defined. In the simplest case, it is the difference of the predicted value and the expected value (the label of the training data). In other cases, slightly more complex functions can be used, but generally quantifying in some way the difference between the predicted value and the expected value.

Training and Test Data

Now we have a model that allows us to classify a text into one of the two categories: positive or negative. But how do we know if the classifier actually performs well? To understand this better, we introduce the concept of *test data*. Assume that we have 100 text samples labeled as positive and 100 labeled as negative. It would be good practice to only use, for example, 80 samples of each category for the training process. 20 positive and 20 negative examples would be kept aside, so that we can *validate* our machine learning classifier on it later. This means that we challenge the classifier to predict whether those snippets are positive or negative, without including them in the training process. This is what we mean when we refer to *unseen data*. Since we know the correct classification for those samples, we can use this knowledge to verify the correctness of our classifier. If it is able to classify 38 of the 40 (20 positive and 20 negative) snippets correctly, we are probably happy with the result. If only 10 out of 40 are correctly classified, we might want to reconsider the steps taken earlier and maybe try other features or adapt our pre-processing steps.[6] Remember that this is a prediction, and it is highly unlikely that we will build a system that is correct in 100% of the cases.

Figure 3.13 gives an overview of the different steps we have been taking to pre-process our text, select features, and finally train and validate the classifier. All these steps are typically needed to prepare machine learning training.

From Machine Learning to Deep Learning

We saw in the previous section how machine learning models are trained: The features were predefined, and the system learned by minimizing the loss function. Let's call this architecture *classical machine learning*.

---

[6] There are also tools and libraries (existing software components) that can support the data engineer in automating some of these steps.

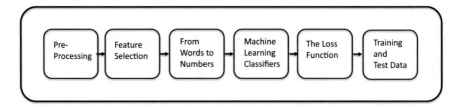

Fig. 3.13 An overview of the different steps needed to prepare for a machine learning training

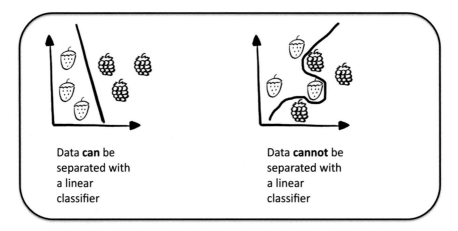

Fig. 3.14 In some cases, the data can be separated with a linear classifier. In other cases, this is not possible

Limitations of Linear Models

Additionally, logistic regression and some other classical machine learning are examples of what are known as *linear models*. For the case of classification, this means that they are only able to separate classes that can be separated by a straight line (or hyperplane in higher dimensions). In other cases, this is not possible, and the data requires nonlinear processing to deliver good results. The two examples are illustrated in Fig. 3.14.

In cases where we know what to look for and can identify and extract the features that are the most useful for distinguishing classes, classical machine learning classifiers such as logistic regression might be likely to perform well. Some other classical machine learning classifiers even allow to process nonlinearly separable data. However, in many cases, it might not be easy to identify the relevant features. For example, remember the case of the classifier where we wanted to differentiate between strawberry and raspberry pictures that we have seen earlier. Whereas for the human eye it is pretty easy to see whether there is a raspberry or strawberry on the picture, it would be pretty hard to formalize what we are seeing and define concrete features in terms a machine learning algorithm could understand. Potential features here could be, for example, whether the berry has seeds on the outside or not. However, it would be pretty hard to instruct the computer explicitly how to translate from pixel values to these features. Applying the same reasoning to texts, a human can read between the lines and understand that somebody is in a bad mood based on an e-mail message. But if you were asked to give clear and precise instructions based on what features helped you notice this, it would be difficult to put it in words. You might say it has to do with the *tone*, but how do you extract the *tone* feature from the text to feed into the machine learning algorithm? Such tasks, where it's hard to identify/extract the relevant features from the data, are where the power of *deep learning* saves the day. Deep learning is a subset of machine learning involving one specific technique: *neural networks*.

Neural Networks

Masato Hagiwara describes a neural network as:

> A generic mathematical model that transforms a vector to another vector. That's it. Contrary to what you may have read and heard in popular media, its essence is simple. (Hagiwara 2021, p. 37)

I like this definition, even though it takes a bit the magic, because it brings it to the point: in the end, it's just math.

As in the previous example using logistic regression, we will need to do preprocessing and finally transform our words into vectors. For now, let's just consider that we already have a numerical representation in the form of vectors from each word in our text.

Like the classical machine learning seen previously, a neural network also relies on a feedback loop to improve the predictions. Very simplified, we can see a neural network as the kind of structure shown in Fig. 3.15.

A neural network can be seen as a more complex structure that includes in the very last part a classical machine learning model, similar to the one that has been described before, as shown in Fig. 3.16. Also here, the learning happens by minimizing the loss. Neural networks can consist of multiple layers. The first layer takes the input data and outputs a new set of features, taken as input by the next layer. After repeating this for all layers, the final layer extracts the features that the classical model can work with. The features extracted at

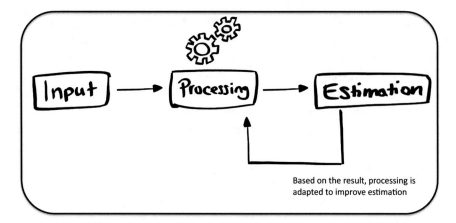

Fig. 3.15 Similar to what we have seen previously for the classical machine learning, neural networks also have a feedback mechanism to improve the predictions

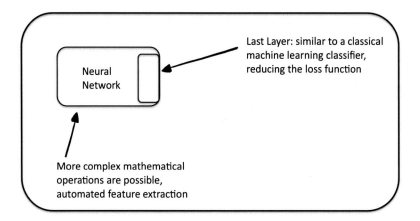

Fig. 3.16 Neural networks are in general similar to classical machine learning, however, allow more complex mathematical operations

each layer can all be modified during training until *the right sequence* of processing steps has been found. When multiple layers are involved in a neural network, we refer to it as *deep learning*. Depending on the exact setup of the neural network, more complex mathematical operations are possible; additionally, the feature extraction can happen automatically, making it often more performant than classical machine learning.

We will now dive a bit deeper into the architectures of neural networks yet staying at a rather high-level.[7]

---

[7] If you are interested in a more mathematical introduction, I can refer you to Rashid (2017), by which some of the examples in this section are inspired by.

Neurons: Inspired by the Human Brain

Neural networks are loosely inspired by the neurons in the human brain. However, we must be clear that such systems are not comparable directly to human brains. They are very simplified, and many aspects of the human brain are still not understood. Consider the following analogy (Rashid 2017): Whereas the human brain has around 100 billion neurons, other smaller animals or insects live with a few hundreds of thousands of neurons. Even though we are able to model computer systems that are much more complex than the brains of those animals, the animals can do some quite useful tasks that would be difficult to solve for a computer. It is worth also mentioning that latest language models have the same order of magnitude of neurons as the human brain. Therefore, the comparison of human or animal intelligence and machine intelligence referring only to the number of neurons is difficult. There seems to be something more to human or animal intelligence.

Coming back to our technical system, a neural network is a set of so-called neurons that are connected to each other. There is a signal that enters on one side of the neural network and passes through the different neurons, and finally, a result comes out.

One layer is typically composed of several neurons. A single neuron, as shown in Fig. 3.17, has several input values and weights assigned to the connections. Inside the neuron, the inputs are processed, and the weights give an indication of how important each input is with regard to the output of the neuron. When thinking about what the weights mean, remember the

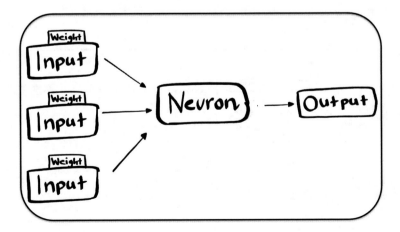

Fig. 3.17   The weights in the neural network are adapted during the training phase to reduce the loss and improve the system's performance

strawberry plant we saw earlier that was bending to the right because of the huge strawberry with a large weight.

The good thing is that we do not have to specify these weights. The weights are adapted during the training phase, to reduce the loss and improve the overall system.

A neural network consists of several neurons, organized in layers.

In the example in Fig. 3.18, we have three layers with two neurons each. The output of the neurons from layer 1 is the input for both neurons of layer 2. Layer 1 is called *input layer*, layer 2 is a *hidden layer* (there could be more than 1), and layer 3 is the *output layer*. In each neuron, computation happens, based on the input values and the weights, and an output is generated. This math is enabled by vector and in particular *matrix*[8] mathematics, and therefore it is important that input and output are vectors and not human words. Such operations can be performed by computers very efficiently even for high-dimensional neural networks.

Learning from Our Mistakes

So how do we learn from mistakes and improve the performance of our neural network? As we did earlier, we want to adapt the weights in order to minimize the loss. If we do this only with the weights in the last layer, as we did for the example of logistic regression (which only had one layer), this fixes the problem only partially. The output of this last layer depends on the input it received from the previous layer. If we don't also adjust the weights there, then we are again in the situation of a low-complexity linear model, so we also need to figure out how to make adjustments to the weights in the second to last layer

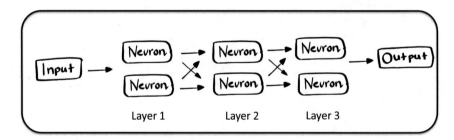

Fig. 3.18 An example of a neural network consisting of three layers

---

[8] A matrix is a table of numbers. For example, a matrix can be multiple vectors being aggregated together. In such a matrix, each column or row of the table would then be a vector.

and so on. We thus have to adapt the weights for each of the layers in the neural network. The process is called *backpropagation*. Figure 3.19 shows how the backpropagation happens in the neural network we have discussed before.

Sentiment Analysis with Neural Networks

Now let's come back to our example of sentiment classification and depict this problem in a neural network. In sentiment analysis, we want to classify texts as negative or positive. For the input, we will need again the vector representations of our words. As shown in Fig. 3.20, the last layer has a special format. Since we aim to have a binary decision, the last neuron is adapted to produce one of these two output options (negative or positive).

As compared to the linear classifiers (such as the logistic regression we have seen previously), neural networks often provide important advantages. For example, the fact that more complex mathematical operations are possible often leads to better performance for text classification. Sometimes, indication for positive or negative sentiment in text can be tricky. Sarcasm might be a strong indicator for a negative sentiment. However, just giving weights to single words as in logistic regression could never capture this complex concept. On the other hand, it is conceivable that some complex function of the combination of words present or not in a text could result in a good measure of sarcasm in text. If so, then neural networks could be able to do this.

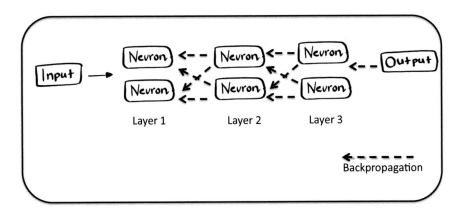

Fig. 3.19 The weights are adapted in all layers of the neural network. This procedure is called backpropagation

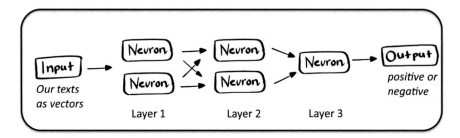

Fig. 3.20 In the context of sentiment analysis on text, we want to provide texts as input and obtain a prediction on whether they are positive or negative

We now have a basic understanding of how neural networks work and are ready to go one step further. In the next section, we will have a closer look at word embeddings, which are vectors that encode the meaning of words.

Diving into Word Embeddings

Let's come back to the problem we have gotten around earlier: the machine learning methods need numerical representations (in the form of vectors) and cannot handle human-readable texts. To enable our text processing and generation with the advantages of machine learning methods, increasing the performance for different tasks, we need to convert the words to mathematical vectors.

So how can we get there? One solution is called *word embeddings*[9] (sometimes also referred to as *word vector*).

Each word from human language, so, for example, the English words *Strawberry* or *Raspberry*, has a numerical representation, a specific word embedding,[10] as shown in Fig. 3.21. Let them be as follows for now:

"Strawberry" = [1,6]
"Raspberry" = [1,7]
"Elephant" = [2,1]

For the sake of example, we consider that our vectors live in a two-dimensional space (therefore, we have two numbers in the brackets above).

---

[9] We could also have *document* embeddings, or *sentence* embeddings, but let's stick for now to the fact that 1 word = 1 vector.

[10] This is similar to the one-hot vectors we have seen previously. However, one advantage with such word embeddings as described here is the lower number of dimensions.

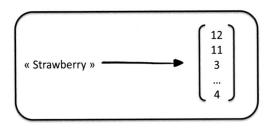

Fig. 3.21 The word "Strawberry" is mapped from human language to a vector

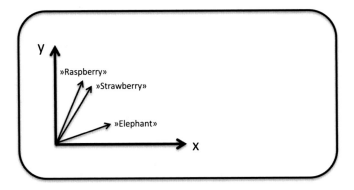

Fig. 3.22 Words that are similar in their meaning have word vectors that are closer together

This means that we are easily able to draw them on a sheet of paper, by using points on a two-dimensional coordinate system.

Relations Between Words

We notice from Fig. 3.22 that the vectors for the words *Strawberry* and *Raspberry* are closer to each other than to the vector of the word *Elephant*. If two words have a similar meaning, their word embeddings will be closer together in the vector space. Since strawberries and raspberries are both berries, as opposed to the elephant being an animal, their word embeddings are closer together. This property allows us to use mathematical operations to deal with the meaning of words. For example, consider the following puzzle (Bolukbasi et al. 2016):

Man is to King, as Woman is to X

This can be solved by using subtractions and additions. Whereas we often use addition or subtraction with numbers (all of us are familiar with doing something like 1 + 2 - 1 = 2), the same can be done also with vectors, leading to the solution of the puzzle[11]:

Vector("Queen") = Vector("King") - Vector("Man") + Vector("Woman")

By subtracting the sum of the vector of the word *man* and the word *woman* from the vector of the word *king*, we can obtain the resulting word *queen*. Fascinating, isn't it?

Similarly, analogy questions can be solved, even across different domains, for example, getting from science to music (Lane et al. 2019):

Who is the Marie Curie of music?

This would translate to vector mathematics as follows, similarly to the example with *king* and *queen* stated above:

Vector("Solution")   =   Vector("Marie   Curie")   -   Vector("Science")   +
Vector("Music")

Naturally, we get very excited and want to explore more relations in these word embeddings and understand how they can be used as input to machine learning training. But where are these word embeddings actually coming from?

Creating Word Embeddings

The main difference between the examples of word embeddings we have seen and actual word embeddings is the dimension.[12] Whereas we used two dimensions in the example to be able to visually look at the word embeddings and their relation among each other, usually they have around 300 dimensions.[13] Hard to imagine? I feel the same way. But the principles we have seen so far

---

[11] Note that the exact values of Vector(«Queen») computed in the example might not exist in the dictionary, and therefore the closest vector to the computed result will most probably be the best solution to the puzzle.

[12] Also, we might likely be dealing with floating point numbers such as 1.2 rather than integers such as 1 or 2.

[13] Typical dimensions are 100 to 500 dimensions, which depends on the corpus (text samples) the word embeddings were trained on (Lane et al. 2019).

are the same: based on the vector's properties and using mathematical operations (they luckily work for different dimensions of vectors), we are still able to obtain the same insights. Why would we use 300 dimensions if we could also use only 2, you might be asking? The intuition behind this is that the more dimensions we have, the more aspects in which words can be similar we can consider. Higher-dimensional vectors help to capture different properties of the words and thus improve the quality of the relations between the word embeddings.

So, let's see how meaning gets encoded into these word embeddings and how we can obtain the word embedding for a specific word in human language. We want to have a dictionary of all words, which translates each word to the corresponding vector. Similar to a language dictionary translating words from English to let's say Spanish, in our case the dictionary is translating words from English to word embeddings. To create such a dictionary, machine learning, or, more precisely, neural networks can be used.

Wait, what? We are using neural networks to generate word embeddings to then use them to encode words that we want to feed to a neural network? Let me explain that more in detail.

We want to convert the words of our text to vectors, in order to process them in a machine learning task, for example, to train a model for a binary classification task in the context of sentiment analysis. This is a supervised machine learning task, since the texts in our training data are labeled as positive or negative. The dictionary of word embeddings is created before that and independently of the actual training process. Those word embeddings can be trained once and reused for different tasks. In the same way as your language dictionary is in your bookshelf, and whenever you need it, for example, to write a letter or translate a word from a text in a foreign language, you just grab it and look up the word you need. The setup is shown in Fig. 3.23.

Word2Vec Embeddings

The dictionary of word embeddings is trained using unsupervised machine learning methods. In this section, we will explore the word2vec method presented in 2013 (Mikolov et al. 2013), which provided major improvements for a range of natural language processing tasks. This was the beginning of a new era of natural language processing with word embeddings, which was later improved even further with transformer-based models, which we will explore in a later chapter.

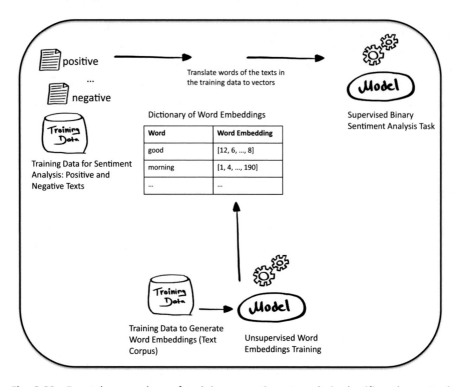

Fig. 3.23 Example procedure of training a sentiment analysis classifier: the textual training data uses existing word embeddings (that have been trained separately) for vectorization

The idea behind the word embeddings can be captured by the following quote from the linguist J.R. Firth:

You shall know a word by the company it keeps (Firth 1962, p. 11)

For example, the word *Strawberry* and the word *Raspberry* might both appear along with the words *berries, field, red, yummy,* and others. Having a common set of words appearing along with them makes it more probable that those two words are similar to each other in terms of meaning. Therefore, the two words should have similar vectors.

The machine learning method to train word embeddings is *unsupervised*. This means that data does not need to be labeled. This is a major advantage in this case because labeling would be complex in the case of natural language. There are many relations and background knowledge that for us, as humans, have been learned over years and would be very difficult to express in a labeled dataset (which would be required when using supervised learning as in the

There is a <u>field</u> <u>with</u> **strawberries** <u>and</u> <u>raspberries</u>.

Fig. 3.24 The word "Strawberry" and the two words that appear just before and just after it

examples before). For example, that a strawberry is a berry and that berries are plants and that plants are eaten by people and animals (and so on).

However, upon closer inspection, the words in a text do have a sort of label. The difference compared to the supervised learning scenario is that labels are available implicitly and do not need to be added before training. Instead of learning the *meaning* of each word, these algorithms learn the common words that appear along with the mentioned word. For this task, the labels for each word in a text are simply the words that appear just before or just after the word itself.[14]

To give you an intuition about what that means, let's look at the example shown in Fig. 3.24. The words *field* and *with* are just before the word *strawberries*, and the words *and* and *raspberries* are right after it. In the skip-gram approach (one of the methods in word2vec word embedding training[15]), we would try to predict the words surrounding each word. In such a case, we use, for example, the words surrounding the word *strawberries* for training. Since we know the correct answers, we can use this information to improve the learning and reduce the error.

To return back to neural networks, the word *strawberries* would be the input to our neural network. As an output, we want the neural network to predict the surrounding words. The neural network for this is structured as shown in Fig. 3.25. We recognize the architecture that we have seen in the previous section: there are neurons and layers. In particular, the input layer consists of the one-hot vector for the word *strawberries*. With the one-hot vector, all fields are 0, and only the field at the position of the specific word in the vocabulary is set to 1. The number of entries in this input layer corresponds to the number of words we have in the vocabulary. In the middle, we have a hidden layer. The hidden layer has a specific number of neurons. The number of neurons corresponds to the number of dimensions the resulting word embeddings should have. In case we would want to produce the sample word embeddings we have seen earlier of two dimensions, then we would have two neurons in this layer. In a more realistic case, where we want to produce word

---

[14] Therefore, this kind of method is also referred to as self-supervised learning.
[15] If you are interested in more details, see Lane et al. (2019, p. 191).

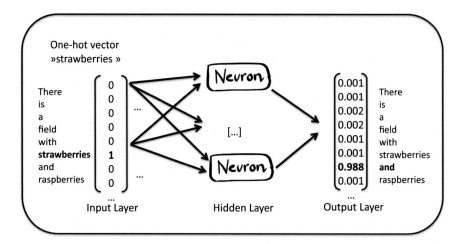

Fig. 3.25 Example about the training of word embeddings (based on Lane et al. (2019, p. 193))

embeddings of 300 dimensions, we would have 300 neurons here. Finally, the output layer outputs a value that corresponds to a probability for each of the words in the vocabulary. In Fig. 3.25, we see the example for the training pair "strawberries+and" (one out of many training steps).

When talking about probabilities, we use values between 0 and 1. Some people are perhaps more familiar with using percentages, but the conversion from probabilities on a 0–1 scale to percentage values is simple. For example, a probability of 0.5 is 50%, and 0.2 is 20%. Based on that, with a probability of 98.8%, the word *and* is very likely to follow the word *strawberries*.

During the training, the pair "strawberry+and" makes the score for *and* go up, while the training example "strawberry+with" would make the score for *with* go up. The training happens in iterations, depending on the number of surrounding words we consider. For example, in the case depicted in Fig. 3.24, we have four surrounding words and thus would need to do four iterations before getting to the next word. Therefore, we might not see the words *and* and *strawberries* being very related in general; however, this is the right answer in this training step.

This procedure is repeated a large number of times. First, we iterate over all words in the sentence, doing one training step for each surrounding word. We then do this not only for a few sentences but for large text corpora including millions of pages of text.

Surprisingly, once the training is done, the output layer can be ignored. What we are actually looking for is in the hidden layer. It generates for each word a vector (the word embedding) encoding the semantics in terms of the other words in the vocabulary it frequently appears with. Words that are semantically similar will have similar vectors. This means that we can extract the word vectors that we need to create our dictionary to map English words to word embeddings from the hidden layer, once the training is concluded.[16]

This is just one procedure for generating word embeddings. In addition to the skip-gram method presented here, Mikolov et al. (2013) also propose an alternative method that works slightly differently, inverting the task to predict a word based on a collection of surrounding words. Other methods are GloVe (Pennington et al. 2014) embeddings or fasttext (Mikolov et al. 2018).

Off-the-Shelf Word Embeddings

As we see in Fig. 3.23, word embeddings can be created once and then reused. This is fortunate, because the training of word embeddings requires a lot of resources. On one side, you need powerful hardware to execute the computations. On the other side, you need to be patient, as such training might take hours or days (or even more in the case of the large language models we will look at in later chapters). Additionally, a large amount of text data (a so-called corpus) is required for the training. Luckily, word embeddings are often publicly available and can be downloaded and used off the shelf by text processing applications. So, when is it worth it to generate your own word embeddings? Since word embeddings are language dependent, you might need to train your own word embeddings for a specific language. However, fasttext (Mikolov et al. 2018) makes word embeddings available in 157 languages (Grave et al. 2018), so this is rarely the case nowadays. In other cases, you might need to train your own embeddings when you need a domain-specific vocabulary. The off-the-shelf word embeddings (as word2vec or fasttext) rely on texts covering a huge range of topics, attempting to model "general" language. But let's say you are working solely with legal documents. Those documents might contain many domain-specific words, and you might be particularly interested in seeing the relations between precisely those words encoded in the word embeddings.

---

[16] For a more detailed explanation about this, refer to Lane et al. (2019, p. 191).

Working with Libraries

In a similar fashion, *libraries* implementing the common methods for machine learning or data preparation tasks are available to data engineers. This means that data engineers, rather than rewriting each time all the instructions in the programming language, can include predefined components in their software. By using the library, the data engineer can provide the input dataset, make specific settings, and then, for example, reuse the logistic regression algorithm implemented by somebody else beforehand. This simplifies the use of these technologies from an applied perspective and shifts the required knowledge to knowing which libraries are available, what they are used for, and how to apply them. Figure 3.26 illustrates the typical components available to the data engineer for model training.

The word embeddings we have seen so far encode one word as one mathematical vector. These encodings can be shared and reused in different applications. More complex language models can also be shared with the community, once trained.

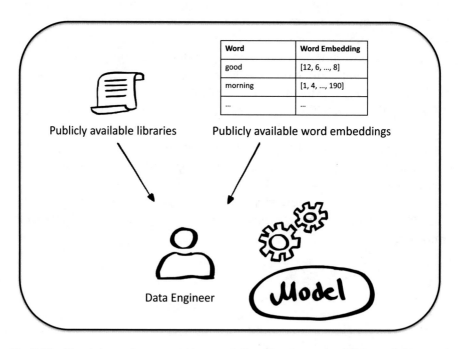

Fig. 3.26 The data engineer can rely on existing libraries and publicly available word embeddings

A High-Level View of Language Models

Looking toward these language models, which we will soon meet, I want to give you a high-level overview at this point of what we are dealing with. Let's for now define *language models* as statistical models that link probabilities to pieces of text. Often, they are, stated in a very simplified way, used to predict the next word in a (partial) sentence, aiming to produce the best human-like text. Let's consider the following example:

Anna goes to the field and collects …

With a language model, we can predict what could be the next word in this sentence. Probably, based on other texts that language models include in their training data, words such as *strawberries, carrots,* or *tomatoes* are more likely to be the next word compared to the words *cats* or *dogs*. The training happens by hiding some words from the original texts and then predicting them. This is somewhat similar to the word embedding training algorithm we saw in this chapter, and so we are well equipped to move toward large language models!

Summary

In this chapter, we learned about applications and methods of natural language processing. We saw how different solutions with varying levels of complexity can be applied to the same problem. The challenge lies in the identification of the most suitable method for the given task.

We saw how neural networks can be beneficial for nonlinearly separable data by allowing more complex mathematical operations and automating feature extraction. Both classical machine learning and deep learning rely on a loss function and adapting the model weights to minimize the loss and improve the model's predictions.

In the context of natural language processing, vectorization is important for mapping human language to mathematical vectors that can be more easily processed by the computer. We have seen different methods for how word embeddings can be trained and how semantically similar words correspond to vectors that are closer together.

Finally, we saw how publicly available word embeddings and libraries are integrated into the data engineer's workflow.

4

Do Chatbots Have Emotions?

Overview

The idea of creating *intelligent* machines has always been a fascination to humanity, resulting in a large variety of books and movies dealing with these kinds of scenarios. With the rise of advanced language models, the question of what we actually mean by *intelligent* comes up once more. In this chapter, we will discuss this matter and see how it is influenced by human perception. In the second part of the chapter, we will deepen our technical skills and look at state-of-the-art language models. Finally, I will describe a typical example of chatbot architecture.

Machines and Emotions

The Turing Test

Already in early years of computer science, in the 1950s, the challenge of measuring whether a machine could have the same thinking capabilities as a human was discussed. A test nowadays referred to as *Turing Test* (originally called *Imitation Game* (Turing 1950)) is often referred to when discussing this topic. In the experiment, a human interacts with a keyboard and a screen with two conversation partners (pretty much like a chatbot conversation nowadays), where one is a human and the other is a machine. The participant is not able to see or hear the two conversation partners. Next, the participant is questioning the two conversation partners, trying to find out who the machine

M. Kurpicz-Briki, *More than a Chatbot*, https://doi.org/10.1007/978-3-031-37690-0_4

is and who the human. Figure 4.1 illustrates this setup. If after an intensive conversation the human is not able to identify who the machine is and who the human, then the test assumes that the machine has the same thinking capabilities as a human.

When having conversations with ChatGPT or similar chatbots based on state-of-the-art language models, the one or other of you might have the impression that this criterion could be fulfilled. Does it mean that we have reached the point of machines having the same thinking capabilities as humans?

The Turing test has been criticized for the fact that it is all about deception that it tests the gullibility of persons rather than the actual intelligence of the system (Tegmark 2018). What is tested in the scenario described above is the ability to write *like* a human, and not performing the thinking or understanding of a human. We can more concretely investigate that by looking at the example of word vectorization we have seen earlier. Based on mathematical operations, we were able to obtain the word *queen* based on the word vectors of the words *king, man*, and *woman*. Does it mean that the system did *understand* the concept of being a king or what is the difference between man and woman? Probably it did not, all it did was to apply mathematical operations on vectors, and the vectors were sorted the way they are in the vector space, due to all the examples seen in the training data.[1]

Emotional Chatbots?

What about the emotions expressed by chatbots? Let's consider the following conversation with a state-of-the-art chatbot (based on a GPT-3 model):

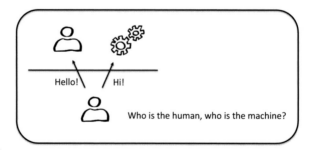

Fig. 4.1   The setup of the Turing Test: who is the human, and who is the machine?

---

[1] We could off course enter the discussion of what human understanding actually is and how it happens, which is beyond the scope of this book. What I want to point out here is that what is happening here in the word embeddings is much simpler than what is potentially happening in the human brain.

Human: "Hello, how are you?"
Chatbot: "Hi, I am doing well. Thank you for asking. How about you? How are you feeling today?"
Human: "I'm OK. A bit low since it's cloudy outside. What is going well for you?"
Chatbot: "I'm sorry to hear that you are feeling a bit low today. It's completely understandable to feel that way when the weather is gloomy. As for me, I am feeling grateful for the people in my life who support me and make me happy. I also feel content knowing that I have the ability to recognize and process my emotions in a healthy way, which helps me to stay mentally and emotionally balanced."

Not bad right? Would this chatbot pass the Turing test? Maybe yes. Does the chatbot *understand* the texts it produces in a way a human would? No, it doesn't.

The fact that this is hard to believe is rooted in the nature of how humans communicate. This was pointed out in detail in a key scientific paper that appeared in 2021 and warned of the dangers and risks behind large language models (Bender et al. 2021). It points out (among many other interesting points that we will discuss later) that the texts generated by large language models are lacking different key aspects of the usual communication pattern between two humans, who share a common ground: communicative intent, a model of the world, and a model of the reader's state of mind. This leads to the problem that even though one side of the communication (the chatbot) has no deeper meaning in the output it produces, humans assume *implicit meaning*, which creates an illusion of our singular human understanding of language. Basically, we are tricked by the chatbot simulating to write like a human.

The way robots, AI and, in particular, also language models process information and present answers or results to humans can be seen as *simulations* of human behavior or activities:

> We have to realize that *thinking, calculating*, the *reactions*, the *decisions* of a robot are only *simulations* of thinking, calculating, reactions, decisions and not – in the human sense – real thinking processes. (Nida-Rümelin and Weidenfeld 2022, p.59)

This fact was in an interview with regard to humanoid robots also referred to as *social hallucinations* by the German philosopher Thomas Metzinger (Honert 2017). He states that humans have the capacity to imagine that they are dealing with a conscious counterpart, even if they are not. This does not only apply with humanoid-looking robots but might also apply to chatbots. In other situations, it can even happen that we assign human characteristics to more passive objects such as cars. For example, a study has shown that people are assigning personality traits or facial expressions to cars (Windhager et al. 2008). In this study, 40 participants were shown 3D computer models from different cars of different manufacturers. The participants were asked to say whether they associate the front part of the cars with a human (or animal) face, identifying the parts that would correspond to mouth, eyes, or other parts of the face. They were furthermore asked to rate to what extent the car looks, among others, happy, angry, surprised, dominant, or sad. Interestingly, people generally agreed in their ratings, and the authors thus assume that there must be some consistent information that is perceived by humans in car fronts. The participants thus evaluated the cars in biological terms, even though being inanimate structures.

The Uncanny Valley

In the case of robots and avatars,[2] being too humanlike leads to negative emotions in humans. It is observed that objects that are clearly artificial and distinguishable from real humans (such as humanoid robots clearly looking different from humans or stuffed animals) are better accepted. The hypothesis of the *uncanny valley* (first proposed in 1970 by the Japanese Robotics Professor Masahiro Mori (Mori 1970)) predicts that an entity appearing almost human on the other hand will cause the feeling of cold and spookiness in humans.

This uncanny valley effect can also be applied to chatbots. A study (Ciechanowski et al. 2019) has observed how two different groups of human participants interact with two groups of chatbots: The first chatbot was a very simple text-based chatbot, and the second one had also an avatar reading the answers rather than only displaying them on the screen. In the results, the authors conclude that the participants were experiencing less uncanny effects and less negative affect when dealing with the simpler chatbot than with the animated chatbot.

It seems that state-of-the-art language models have not only enabled a revolution in the field of natural language processing, making several tasks more efficient. They furthermore seem to raise new questions of human-chatbot

---

[2] The term *avatar* in general refers to electronic images or animations of humans or artificial characters, which are used in the virtual world (Internet, video games, virtual reality, etc.).

interaction, leading us to interpret their eloquent and well-phrased texts as emotions or making us feel eerie when interacting with them. Has some sort of language model uncanny valley been reached?

You are still thinking about the over-emotional chatbot conversation and not convinced it is only an illusion? Let's now get back to the technical part now and have a closer look at how chatbots work and how their answers are generated.

Entering the World of Language Models

Vectors of Entire Sentences

So far, when looking at word embeddings, we have considered settings where one word corresponds to one vector. Each word in our example had one numerical representation, being of two dimensions for the toy example and of larger dimensions in the real-world word embeddings. In some cases, it might be necessary or preferable to aggregate several words together. When doing sentiment analysis of texts, often we would like to understand whether an entire sentence (or blocks of text) is positive or negative, rather than just the individual words. When doing this type of operation on sentences and using a machine learning model that takes entire sentences as input, we have a *sentence classification task*. Other examples of similar tasks are a spam filter or identifying whether a given text is about a specific topic.

Consider the following sentence, which we want to feed to a machine learning model and estimate whether it is positive or negative:[3]

Anna eats a tasty strawberry.

Based on the word embeddings discussed earlier, we can now easily encode each word as a vector:[4]

Vector("Anna") = (0, 2)
Vector ("eats") = (1, 3)
…

---

[3] Inspired by the example of Hagiwara (2021)
[4] As before, for the sake of the example, we are using only two dimensions.

We now want to aggregate these word embeddings to a so-called sentence embedding, a vector representing not only a single word but the entire sentence. One simple method to do so is to just take the average of all word vectors in the sentence. Based on the mathematical properties of vectors, we can apply mathematical operations, as if we could be taking the average of numbers:

Average = [Vector("Anna")+Vector("eats")+...+Vector("strawberry")]/5

We sum up all the vectors and divide by the number of vectors (= the number of words). The result is one vector (in the same dimension as the word vectors) that represents the entire sentence:

Vector("Anna eats a tasty strawberry.")

These methods also help to deal with the handling of *sequences of variable-length*. When dealing with language, words (which can be seen as *sequences* of characters) can be longer (as the word *strawberry*) or shorter (as the word *the*). In the same way, we can see sentences as a *sequence* of words, and the number of words per sentence can vary. Therefore, we can consider a sentence that we want to provide as input to our machine learning model as a *variable-length input*. Depending on the sentence we want to classify, we might have less or more words to process. Mostly, we will not be able to know this information in advance and thus need to be ready in our software to process very short sentences, as well as long sentences. Using the average is a simple yet efficient solution to that: no matter how many words there are in the sentence, we will end up with a single vector (of fixed dimension).

Whereas this solution solves our problem for now, it comes with some major limitations. For instance, the order in which the words appear in the sentence is not considered when using this method. This results in the following sentence having the same sentence vector as our example above:

A tasty strawberry eats Anna.

Not quite the same, right? In some cases, this difference can be very relevant for the classification task, and thus, we need more advanced methods that allow to consider the order of the words in the sentence. Additionally, the longer a sentence is, the less information the average vector contains.

Keeping Some Words in Mind

To overcome this limitation, we need a different approach that allows us to keep in mind the order of words, by reading them step by step from left to right, as a human reader would do. Let's consider this by an example[5] as shown in Fig. 4.2.

We consider the same example sentence from before. The human reader reads the sentence word by word.[6] As a first step, the word *Anna* is read and stored in the short-term memory. Then, the next word, in this case *eats*, is read. It is put in context with the words that have already been read before and is stored in the short-term memory as well. Here, the short-term memory is updated and becomes "Anna eats," taking note about the relation of the two words, meaning that there is an action that was executed by Anna. This short-term memory can also be referred to as a *mental state*, that is, updated step by step based on the new words that are being read while going through the sentence word by word (Hagiwara 2021).

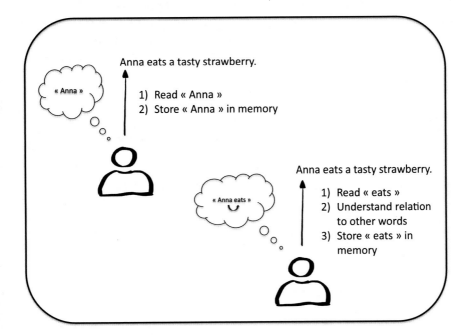

Fig. 4.2 Example of a human reading a sentence word by word (based on the explanations of Hagiwara (2021))

---

[5] Inspired by the examples of Hagiwara (2021)

[6] This might be too simplified from a cognitive science point of view but aims at helping us understand better the coming technical explanations.

Neural Networks with Loops

We now want to bring together this mechanism of reading a sentence and the neural networks that we saw in the previous chapter. These neural networks are called *recurrent neural networks* (*RNNs*). We can translate the human reader's process in the previous example to a more technical setup as follows: We introduce the concept of the *state* of a neural network as an analog for the short-term memory of the reader, updating it after each word vector in a similar manner, as shown in Fig. 4.3.

To begin, the neural network receives the vector of the word *Anna*. It then receives the second vector: the vector of the word *eats*. This vector is combined with the output of the hidden layer from the previous step and passed to the next step. In other words, the state of the neural network is updated, reflecting the additional information that the new word brings to the entire sentence read so far. This operation is repeated until the end of the sentence has been reached. By then, the content of the entire sentence is stored in this *final state*.

In the previous chapter, we have seen the neural network architecture, consisting of an input layer, several hidden layers, and an output layer. Each layer consisted of several neurons, which were each processing an input and some weights and providing an output to the next layer. You might remember that

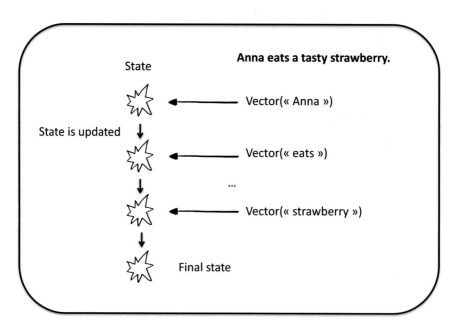

Fig. 4.3 A neural network processing a sentence vector by vector (based on the explanations of Hagiwara (2021))

a signal was entering our neural network from the input layer and making all its way layer by layer to the output layer. Since when reading a sentence word by word, we perform the same operations again and again, the same neural network structure is being re-used. There are *loops* in the processing. Loops are a common construct in computer programming. Whenever the same operation needs to be executed numerous times, specific constructs can be used to write the instruction only once and tell the computer to execute it several times. This is analogous to the following scenario: If you have ten bowls of strawberries and want to instruct somebody to bring them all from the kitchen to the table in the living room, you could either say:

Please go to the kitchen and bring the first bowl of strawberries to the table.
Then, please go again to the kitchen and bring the second bowl of strawberries to the table.
and so on.

However, you would probably not be doing that. You would be saying something like:

For each of the ten bowls, please go to the kitchen and bring the bowl to the table.

So, you just created a loop with ten iterations.

The idea of reusing a neural network in a loop structure gives rise to the concept of so-called recurrent neural networks. The same structure can be reused as the next word comes in. At each step, we take the hidden layer output from the previous iteration (the state) along with the word vector of the current step as input into the network. It allows the neural network to connect the incoming word to the rest of the sentence. Coming back to the strawberry bowls in the kitchen, the person picking up the bowls could have a notebook and a pen in the kitchen, taking note each time which bowls were already taken to the table and how they were placed.

The architecture of our recurrent neural network therefore looks as shown in Fig. 4.4. The *state* corresponds to the short-term memory mentioned earlier and stores information about each word's context.

Why is this useful? Suppose we want to generate text by predicting the next word of a partial sentence:

Step 1:   Anna eats …
Step 2:   Anna eats a …
Step 3:   Anna eats a strawberry …

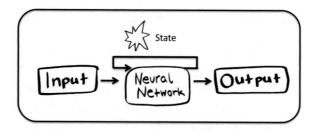

Fig. 4.4 The architecture of a recurrent neural network

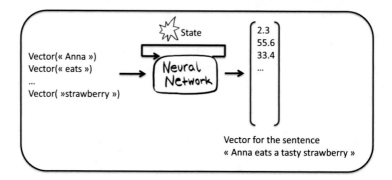

Fig. 4.5 A recurrent neural network generating a vector for a complete sentence

The word generated at each step is given by the neural network's prediction for the next word. In each of the steps, the same neural network is used, and the state is the output of the hidden layer, which stores information about everything seen so far.

So, let's come back to our initial problem. We wanted to find a better way than the averaging method to produce a fixed-length vector from a variable-length input. And with recurrent neural networks, we have found a solution. As shown in Fig. 4.5, we can input a sentence (each word encoded as a vector) and get a sentence embedding by using this type of neural network. The sentence embedding is the final state of the neural network. Thanks to the repetition that is possible by using the loop inside the neural network, we can use it for very short sentences as well as sentences containing many words. Furthermore, as advantage over the averaging method, the order of the words in the sentence is considered here.

Often, we will find a visual representation as shown in Fig. 4.6 to illustrate the same network. Instead of the loop, the recurrent neural network is *unfolded* and displayed as several identical layers. This can be beneficial, as it allows to display how the sequence of words (the sentence) is processed step by step.

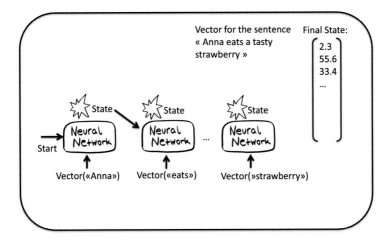

Fig. 4.6   Unfolded representation of the recurrent neural network

The state of each copy of the neural network represents the information about the words that has been introduced up to that point.

Here They Are, the Language Models!

We are now approaching the heart of this book, introducing the concept of language models. Let's look at the following definition:

> Formally, a language model is a statistical model that gives a probability to a piece of text. […] The more grammatical and the more "sense" the sentence makes, the higher the probability is. (Hagiwara 2021, p. 131)

Let's consider the following two sentences:

There is a field full of strawberries.
There is a field full of cats.

With our world and language knowledge, it is easy to determine for a human that the first sentence is much more likely than the second sentence. This feeling of *being likely* is expressed in probabilities in language models. For the sentences above, we would expect a language model to give a *higher probability* to the first sentence and a lower probability to the second one.

Language models are the foundation of many natural language processing tasks. Examples range from machine translation to speech recognition and answer generation in chatbots.

Put simply, to get the probability of the sentence, the probabilities of each word under consideration of the context (the words before and/or after it) are combined. For example, consider the following sentence:

There is a field full of strawberries.

We would consider questions like: How likely is it that a sentence starts with *There*? How likely is it that the word *is* comes after the word *There*? The answers to all these questions would provide us an overall probability, which could then be compared with the overall probability of another sentence, to decide which of the sentences is more likely to be a *real, good* sentence (a combination of words that a human is likely to use).

When looking at these questions, you might have recognized some similarity to the task before, where we created the sentence embeddings. To generate the sentence embeddings, we were processing the sentence word by word, considering also the context and storing the meaning in our *state*. To answer the questions about *likeliness* raised in the previous paragraph, we also need to process the sentence word by word and consider the probability of the word being in a given position of the sentence.

We can thus use the architecture of a recurrent neural network and train our first language model.

To start, we return to the unfolded recurrent neural network we have seen previously. In particular, we are now interested in the intermediate values of the *state*. When looking at this without the output in Fig. 4.7, we realize that we actually do the following: based on a sequence of inputs (sequence of words in form of vectors), we generate a sequence of outputs (the intermediate values of state). Such an architecture is called *sequence-to-sequence encoder*.

Whereas the intermediate values of the *state* are useful, it is not what we want as output for our language model. What we want is an indication of the probability of potential next words, based on the partial sequence (the partial sentence) we have read so far.

In Fig. 4.8, we consider the example of reading the first word of the sentence, *Anna*. The output of this step is the probability of the next word. Whereas it is very likely that the word *Anna* is followed by the word *eats*, it is rather unlikely that it is followed by *strawberry* or *tasty*. As in the previous chapter, we express probabilities as numbers ranging from 0.0 to 1.0 that can be easily mapped to percentages of 0% to 100%.

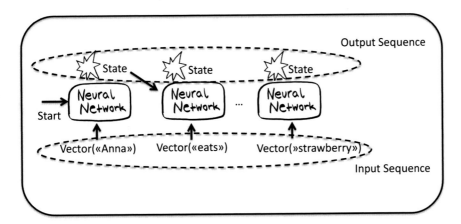

Fig. 4.7 The architecture of a sequence-to-sequence encoder

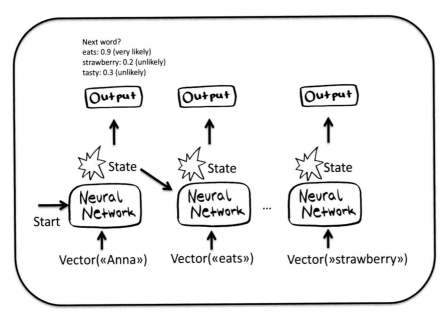

Fig. 4.8 The word following the word "Anna" in the sentence is predicted. Whereas the word "eats" seems to be likely a good choice, the words "strawberry" and "tasty" have lower probabilities

As stated before, we want to use this architecture to *train* the language model. We are thus applying the above principle to a large number of texts, *hiding* specific words and predicting them, in order to be able to control and adjust the result as needed. Reducing the loss here means getting closer to correctly predicting the hidden words.

In the example above, we know that the word *eats* follows the word *Anna* in our text. Thus, *eats* is the correct answer, for which, in a fully trained system (in the prediction phase), we expect to have the highest probability. However, in the beginning of the training phase, it would be likely that maybe the answer is not correct yet, and the model is estimating higher probabilities for other words. And this is where the learning happens: based on the estimated values at this step, and the correct answer, an *improvement* of the system to make better predictions happens (this happens as we have seen before by adapting the weights inside the neural network to minimize the loss), sentence by sentence, text by text, for millions or billions of words.

Once the language model has been trained, we can use it to construct new sentences! This occurs in the *prediction phase*. By providing the first part of the sentence, we can make a prediction of the next word, as shown in Fig. 4.9. We ask the language model to predict the next word in the sentence "Anna eats a tasty …", and (hopefully) the answer of our language model is *strawberry*. Behind the scenes, there is again a probability score for every word in the vocabulary leading to this answer.

The main difference between the training of the word embeddings earlier and this procedure is the input. In the training of the word embeddings, we were calculating the probability of a word being a context word to the target word (the word being encoded). The only input was the target word. In the case of the neural networks in this section, the input to predict the probability of a next word considers not only one word but the previous state, which included information about several words.

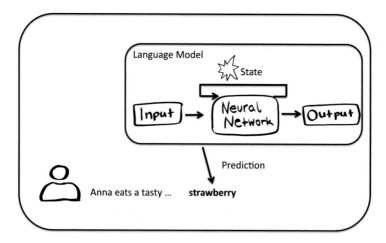

Fig. 4.9 Using a language model to predict the next word in a sentence

We now have seen how to build a language model by using a recurrent neural network as a first example of a sequence-to-sequence encoder. That's an achievement, congratulations!

Toward Transformer Models

There is now only one last step left to bring us to the latest state-of-the-art language models. Current models such as Google's BERT (Devlin et al. 2019) or GPT-3 or GPT-4 from OpenAI are so-called transformer-based models (Vaswani et al. 2017). We will discover in this section what this architecture looks like and why it is so powerful.

We saw in the previous section how we can create a language model that can generate text by predicting the next word in a partial sentence. In the example, we observed the transformation from a sequence of words (a sentence) to a sequence of probabilities (which is the most likely next word?). Now, we would like to slightly adapt the use case and transform a sequence of words to *another* sequence of words. This could be a sentence in English as input, which is translated to another sentence in Spanish, or the question of a user to a chatbot, which is transformed to the matching answer. To achieve this, we will connect two models as the one seen before and transform a sequence of text to another sequence of text. In particular, we will deal with a question-answering task in this section.

Encoders and Decoders

To illustrate the idea, let's consider the following query a user might ask to a chatbot:

In what countries do strawberries grow?

To generate an answer, we need to process this user input and find the most appropriate answer. This assumes that the training process of the model was already concluded, and we are in the prediction phase here. Let's assume for our example that the chatbot will generate the following (not so help-ful) answer:

Strawberries grow in different countries.

To do that, we use one model to create a sentence embedding of the first sentence and then pass it to another model and use this second model to generate the answer. The first model is called *encoder*, as it encodes the meaning of the input sentence in a sentence embedding (a vector representation of the entire sentence). The second model is called *decoder*, as it decodes this embedding and generates the answer sentence. Figure 4.10 shows the high-level view of this architecture.

Based on what we have seen previously, we can have a closer look now what happens inside these two components – the encoder and the decoder. The way such sequence-to-sequence models can be implemented can vary: depending on the specific natural language processing task, the encoder or decoder can be implemented differently.

Let's create an encoder that is based on the recurrent neural network architecture we have seen previously to generate the sentence embeddings. The sentence embedding corresponded to the hidden state after the final iteration. This network is actually already doing the task of the encoder, so we can just take it from the previous section and include it as encoder in this new system.[7] Phew, first step is done!

Let's now look at the decoder. Whereas in the previous example, the estimation of the next word was based on the context of the words that had been generated so far, for the decoder, the input the model receives from the encoder is considered as well. Based on that, the output sentence is generated, word by word, as shown in Fig. 4.11.

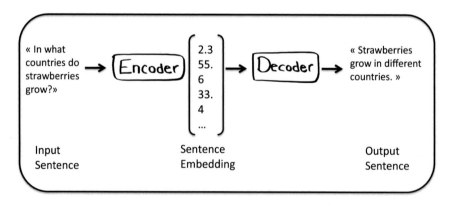

Fig. 4.10 A high-level view of the encoder-decoder architecture

---

[7] The architecture is slightly different in the transformer model presented in Vaswani et al. (2017). The neural network does not contain loops, and information goes from the input layer through the hidden layer to an output layer. We will discuss this in a few pages.

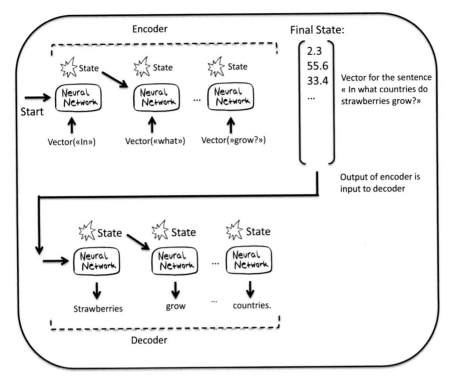

Fig. 4.11 A more detailed view on the two parts of the encoder-decoder architecture. The output of the encoder is the input to the decoder

Pre-Training and Fine-Tuning

Let's now look more in detail into the training process of our question answering task. The training phase for this example has two parts. We assume that we have a recurrent neural network as seen previously that was already *pre-trained*. This means that it was already trained with a large corpus of text, and thus the weights are already configured to quite good values. In general, it is ready to make predictions about the next word in a sentence. We take two instances of this model: one we will use to encode our sentences (encoder) and the other one to generate the answer text (decoder). We prepare a dataset to *fine-tune* this model. In an additional training phase, with additional training data, the weights are optimized further. In particular, since the model was trained in general for text generation, the fine-tuning allows to specialize for a specific task, in our case, the question answering.

Table 4.1 shows an example on how the training data for this fine-tuning could look like.

Table 4.1 Example of the training data for the fine-tuning task

Question	Answer
<START> In what countries do strawberries grow? <END>	<START> Strawberries grow in different countries. <END>
<START> Which color do strawberries have? <END>	<START> With exceptions, strawberries are mostly red <END>
…	…

Let's define *tokens* as common sequences of characters found in text.[8] We will consider in the following examples entire words as input tokens. In reality, not every word necessarily matches exactly one token. For example, the word *sequences* is split in two tokens: *sequ* and *ences*.

In the context of our encoder-decoder architecture, one aspect to consider is the length of words in the input and the output. Naturally, the question from the user to the chatbot and the answer from the chatbot can have a different number of words. Special words, so-called special tokens, are used to mark the beginning (<START>) and the end (<END>) of an input or output sequence.

The question and the answers with these special tokens are shown in Table 4.1. Of course, we would need a long list of these question-and-answer pairs to fine-tune the language model.

In the fine-tuning process, the first question is fed to the encoder, generating the sentence embedding. The decoder receives the output of the encoder (the sentence embedding). Since we are in the fine-tuning, which is part of the training phase, we know the answer sentence to this question from our training data. The first word is thus generated, and the learning has the aim to maximize the probability for the word we are looking for. However, in the beginning, other words will be proposed. The system still has to learn. In a next step, when generating the second word of the answer sentence, we take as input the sentence embedding received from the encoder and the first word of the *correct* answer. On purpose, we refer to the correct answer, and not to the word generated in the first step of the learning, as it might be wrong during the learning process and create misleading information for the estimation of the following words. For each generated word, the difference between that word and the correct answer is considered to improve the system. Again, we want to adapt the weights in order to reduce the loss. As before, the system improves over many iterations and many training examples, repeating the steps mentioned in this paragraph.

---

[8]To see how a sentence is tokenized in the GPT family of models, see https://platform.openai.com/tokenizer.

Once the system has been fine-tuned and is applied to new user queries where we do not know the correct answer, we are in the prediction phase (or in this case, actually more a *generation* phase). The decoder now works slightly differently than explained for the training phase. Again, the output of the encoder and the <START> token get the whole thing started. In contrast to the training phase, now the predicted word from the previous position is considered to generate the next word (there is no right answer that could be taken anyways, because we are assuming this input is a new question that was not seen during training).

So, now that we have the sequence-to-sequence model up and running and know how encoders and decoders work, we can finally get to the transformer models.

Transformer Models Architecture Overview

The transformer models that were initially presented in 2017 (Vaswani et al. 2017) are a new type of encoder-decoder neural network and started in the field of natural language processing the "era of the transformer" (Hagiwara 2021, p. 185), providing remarkable improvement for different text processing and text generation tasks.

Compared to the encoder-decoder architecture we saw in detail, the transformer-based models are *more of the same*. In these systems, different layers of encoders and decoders are combined. Multiple encoder layers are thus passed through to further improve the results. Whereas in the original paper presenting this architecture six layers were used, it can be many more in practice (Hagiwara 2021). Similarly, the decoder consists of different layers. The architecture is illustrated in Fig. 4.12.

Figure 4.13 shows in more detail what is inside each encoder and decoder component of the transformer model.

As opposed to the example we have seen in detail before, the transformer model does not use recurrent neural networks. Recurrent neural networks and their states have progressively more problems with dependencies between tokens that are far away from each other, the longer the sentences get (Hagiwara 2021). In other words, the state starts to *forget* information about words that occurred much earlier in the sequence. These long-range dependencies can be covered much better when using a mechanism called *self-attention* instead. The transformer applies this self-attention multiple times, in combination with a *feed-forward neural network*. A feed-forward neural network does not have loops, such as the recurrent neural network, and

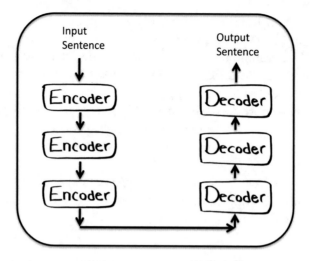

Fig. 4.12 A high-level view of the transformer architecture

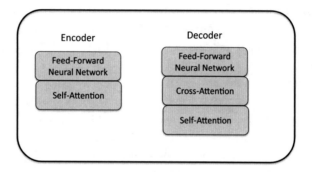

Fig. 4.13 The inner life of the encoder and decoder in the transformer architecture (inspired by the excellent visualization of transformer models from Alammar (2018))

corresponds thus roughly to the very initial type of neural networks we have seen. Going through different layers, the input goes from the left to the right through in the neural network, and finally, an output is produced.

This *attention mechanism* is probably the most important component of what makes the difference of the transformer-based architecture compared to previous natural language processing approaches. We will explore it in more detail in the next sections.

Self-Attention

When looking at the encoder-decoder architecture of sequence-to-sequence models, we notice the high relevance of the sentence embeddings that relate the encoder with the decoder. This vector includes all the information available from the user query to generate the answer from the chatbot. However, this vector is rather limited. Even though it contains some hundred dimensions, it is of *fixed length*. And fixed length might not fit well to all the use cases we might encounter. Whether the input sentence is of 3 words or 20 words, the available space to represent all this information is always the same. Indeed, it is the case that in an architecture as we have seen it before, the performance suffers when the input sentence is very long. This problem could be mitigated if there were some mechanisms to only consider the most important (and not just the most recent as in the case of the RNN) parts of a long sequence. Thus, in summary, we can conclude that the decoder needs more information to refer to different aspects of the input it receives from the encoder. And this is what *self-attention* provides.

For intuition: we want it to concentrate on the most relevant information. Imagine you are looking at a page of text and are asked to spot where the word *strawberry* appears in the text. Automatically, we will scan the text and leave out other information, trying to *focus* on the words relevant for our task. Similarly, we want the transformer model to focus on the relevant information for each given word.

Rather than having a sentence embedding with a fixed-length vector to contain all the information relevant to the input sentence, we return to word embeddings. Each word from the input sentence will have one embedding. However, there is an important difference between the word embeddings we have seen earlier and the word embeddings here. The word embeddings here contain information about the entire context of the word.

To generate these *context-based summaries* for each word is the task of the self-attention mechanism. One could say that based on the word embedding representing a word in form of a vector, a more advanced word embedding is created representing both the word *and* its context.

When computing these advanced word embeddings using self-attention for a given word, each other word in the same sentence is attributed a weight. The weight determines how relevant it is to the given word, like the relevance of the huge strawberry to make the strawberry plant bend, always the same story.

Let's consider the following example:

*There is a field of strawberries, and **it** is so beautiful!*

When using self-attention to compute the context-based summary for the word *it*, the weight for the word *field* would be expected to be higher as for other words, since *it* is referring to the field of strawberries. Using this mechanism of self-attention, we do not lose track of words referring to other words that have appeared previously in the sentence. This is a typical problem of systems not using self-attention, especially when the sentence gets long, and there are many words between the word and the reference to that word.

For example, the attention weights and thus dependencies from the word *it* to the context words could be visualized in a simplified manner as in Fig. 4.14.

Words directly relating to the word *it*, such as the word *field* it refers to, or the word *beautiful* describing it, are more important for its context-dependent summary. Other words, such as *of strawberries* or the verb *is* referring to the word *it*, are relevant but maybe less important than the other words. Therefore, they have smaller weights.

The context-dependent summaries are created and processed in the encoder. As shown in Fig. 4.15, the word *In*, under the consideration of the context, results in one vector that is passed from the encoder to the decoder. With context we mean, for example, the fact that the word *In* is followed by the word *which*, which is followed by the word *countries*. The second vector would be the context-aware representation of the word *which*, the second word of the input sentence and so on for the rest of the words in the input sentence.

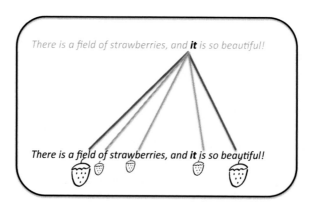

Fig. 4.14 The dependencies from the word "it" reflected in the different weights attributed to different words

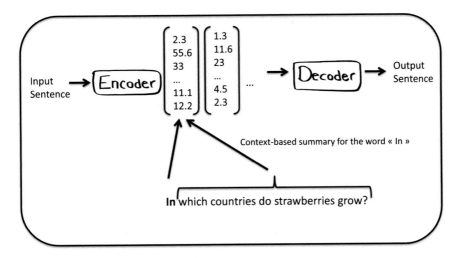

Fig. 4.15   The context-based summaries are created and processed in the encoder

Cross-Attention and Positional Encoding

In the decoder, another form of attention is used: *cross-attention*. This mechanism is similar to the self-attention used inside the encoder and the decoder to generate the context-aware word embeddings. Cross-attention is used in the decoder to summarize the information obtained from the encoder (*cross* in the sense that is crosses the border between encoder and decoder). The idea is here again to obtain the most relevant information under consideration of the context.

When reading about the self-attention mechanism primarily focusing on how words are related, you might have been wondering if we do not have the same problem here as earlier in the book that we miss information about the order of the words (remember the example whether *Anna eats the strawberry* or *the strawberry eats Anna* was represented in the same way). Actually, this could be a problem in the described approach. However, the transformer encoders take care of this by an additional calculation: the *positional encoding*.

The positional encoding is an additional component that is added to the word embedding of a word and contains information about the position. The positional encoding of the word *Anna* in *Anna eats a strawberry* (Anna is in position 1) would be different from the positional encoding of *Anna* in *The strawberry eats Anna* (where Anna is in position 4).

Including information about the position of a word in the calculations of the contextualized word embeddings, this information can be kept, and we are safe from problems such as the strawberry eating Anna.

Static and Contextualized Word Embeddings

The word embeddings we have seen earlier in the book, and that do not consider the context of a word, are also referred to *static* or *traditional word embeddings*. More advanced embeddings as the ones resulting from the transformer-based models seen in this section are referred to as *contextualized word embeddings*. In static word embeddings, the word *orange* referring to the color and the same word *orange* referring to the fruit would be encoded in the same word embedding. In contextualized word embeddings, this would be different, as the context where these words appear in the training data would be considered. For example, the fruit could appear along with strawberries, apples, or bananas, whereas the color could appear along with other colors such as purple, blue, or green. This difference would be considered and reflected in the embeddings when training a transformer-based model. Therefore, the contextualized word embedding of orange (the color) would be different from the embedding for the other orange (the fruit).

These language models we have trained using the transformer architecture can be used as foundation to predict sentences in different situations, like chatbots or next sentence prediction. The language models, or more precisely the *contextualized word embeddings* resulting from these training processes, can also be applied in different other tasks like classification. This reminds us of the dictionary that maps words from human language to vector representations we have seen earlier in this book. As for this dictionary, transformer-based language models can be trained once and then be shared and used in different use cases, as shown in Fig. 4.16. This is good news, because training a state-of-the-art transformer-based model requires powerful (and thus expensive) hardware, large corpora of texts (we talk about thousands of millions of words), and (depending on your hardware) patience for the training to be executed over days or weeks or months.

Before these word embeddings and language models appeared in the landscape of natural language processing, a machine learning model was often trained for one very specific task. As mentioned here and previously, these *pre-trained components* (language models or word embeddings) can be made available and readily used, which has changed the way how natural language processing applications are being built lately. This is an advantage, because different natural language processing tasks may find it beneficial to know that raspberries and strawberries are somewhat similar, because they are both berries. A wonderful analogy to describe this setup has been provided by (Hagiwara 2021):

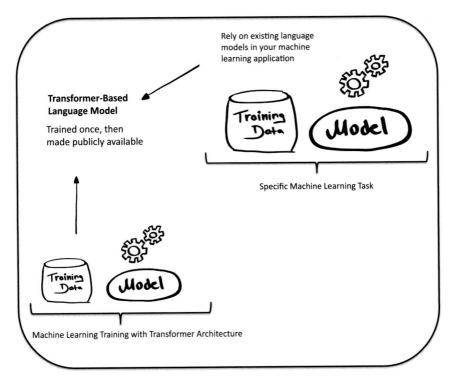

Fig. 4.16 Transformer-based models can be trained and made available to be used in other applications

[This compares to] teaching a baby (=NLP Model) how to dance. By letting babies learn how to walk steadily first (=training word embeddings), dance teachers (=task specific datasets and training objectives) can focus on teaching specific dance moves without worrying whether babies can even stand and walk properly. (Hagiwara 2021, p. 220)

This process of using pre-trained components and adapting them to the needs of the actual task (a process called *adaption* or *fine-tuning*) can generally be referred to as *transfer learning*. The insights from the first learning phase, which are stored inside the language model or the word embeddings, can thus be *transferred* to a different type of task. This avoids training models over and over again from scratch, when it is possible to benefit from already existing language models.

This usually leads the data engineer to have a setup as described in Fig. 4.17. It relies on publicly available word embeddings or language models that have been trained on a large amount of data and can be included easily in the data engineer's project by using libraries. Based on these components and a smaller

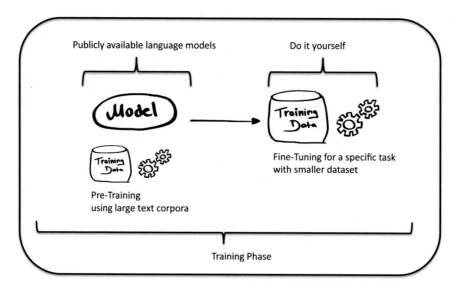

Fig. 4.17 Pre-trained language models can be fine-tuned for other machine learning tasks

training dataset, the fine-tuning procedure does the machine learning training for the actual required task, for example, the sentiment analysis task described earlier. In terms of weights, training from scratch means that we are starting the training phase with random weights. In the case of fine-tuning, the weights have been already learned from a different task and are just adjusted from there.

Having the language models and word embeddings readily available is convenient; however, there are also limitations in them (e.g., bias) that are easily propagated this way. We will discuss more about this in a later chapter.

The BERT Model

As an example, let's have a closer look on which tasks Google's language model BERT was trained (Devlin et al. 2019). The BERT model has been trained on two tasks: *masked language modeling* and *next sentence prediction*. Let's see what that means. For the masked language modeling, 15% of the tokens were hidden in the training data (a large text corpora). The transformer-model had then to predict those masked tokens. This is similar to examples we have seen before. The token <MASK> indicates the word that was covered and needs to be predicted.

There is a field full of <MASK>.

In the second task, the focus was on the relation between different sentences. This is not covered in the first task, relying only on words within one sentence. The system had to predict for two sentences A and B whether sentence B is the sentence that followed sentence A in the original text. In 50% of the cases, this was true, and in 50% of the cases, it was not the case. Consider the following example, where the system would be expected to predict that sentence B is following sentence A:

Sentence A: Anna goes to the field of strawberries.
Sentence B: She collects many berries and takes them home.

In the following example, the system should rather predict that it is not the case:

Sentence A: Anna goes to the field of strawberries.
Sentence B: Cats like to sleep.

The name BERT stands for Bidirectional Encoder Representations from Transformers. This powerful system based on the transformer architecture introduced important advances to the field of natural language processing in 2019.

The Architecture of a Chatbot

Based on what we have seen so far, we can now draw the architecture of a state-of-the-art transformer-based chatbot. As shown in Fig. 4.18, there are different software components involved. In particular, we find the language model with the transformer architecture in the background. As we have seen previously, it consists of different layers of encoders and decoders. Usually, in that kind of applications, there is another software component that allows the human to interact with the language model. This human wanting to interact with software we usually refer to as *the user*. The expectation of the user is in general to have a *graphical user interface* to interact with the software. The community of users wanting a window with black background and small white font without any graphical illustrations is very small and probably limited to a very technical population. You might know this kind of applications from movies, when hackers or critical system shutdowns are involved. In general, users prefer something more graphical, that is, intuitive to use. In the case of a chatbot, this is often provided by a *web application*. A web

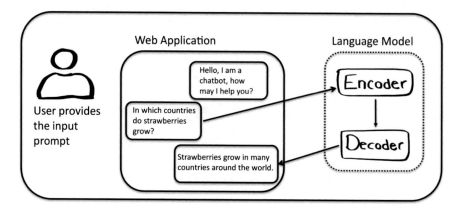

Fig. 4.18 The architecture of a chatbot: often web applications are used as an interface between the user and the language model

application can be launched by the user by opening a link in their web browser or by installing an application on their smartphone. Typically, when opening the conversation with the chatbot, they will receive a greeting message and are then able to enter their *input prompt*. This input prompt will be processed by the language model, and the answer sentence will be produced, using the methods we have seen earlier. The sentence that is returned is *most probably* a good answer to the question that the user entered the input prompt. How good it really is depends on the input data and training setup of the language model.[9]

Finally, in some setups, the user is also used as a *trainer* for the language model. It is possible to gather feedback from users to improve the language model's prediction or make them safer. For example, the user can rate the answer, saying whether it was useful or not. In other cases, we would want to flag specific types of answers as inappropriate. The more input and corrections from human trainers are achieved, the better the system can adapt.

That's it. Now we understand how state-of-the-art language models and chatbots work. Let's now get back to the example conversation of the chatbot exposing its emotions that we have seen earlier in this chapter.

At a first sight, it seemed counterintuitive that there is no understanding or meaning in a human-sense behind the texts produced by the chatbot, given the fluent and eloquent way it phrases its answers. The answers seemed coherent and pronounced spontaneously and naturally. When considering the technical background and the generation of the most likely next word based

---

[9] Note that there are different ways how language models in combination with chatbots can be implemented. We are referring here to an example based on the architecture stack we have seen before.

on probabilities, you might want to reconsider the option that these languages' models reason and produce text in the same way that you do.

The philosophical debate about what consciousness, reasoning, or intelligence mean in a deeper sense, and whether this can be achieved with materials other than the human brain, is not part of this book. I want to give you a basic understanding of how language models work and that they are (currently) not comparable to the capacities of human reasoning, not having mental states like beliefs, desires, intentions, or fears. As argued by Nida-Rümelin and Weidenfeld (2022, p. 17), "digital states and processes *simulate* mental ones but are not identical to them, even if that simulation were perfect."

Summary

In this chapter, we have discussed whether chatbots can have emotions. We have seen that even though the texts they produce are often eloquent and empathic, behind the scenes, it is more about the prediction of the most likely next word, based on probabilities.

We have also learned what recurrent neural networks are and how we can build sequence-to-sequence models from them using an encoder-decoder architecture. Based on that, we understood how the transformer architecture works and how self-attention enables efficient state-of-the-art language models. We have also explored how pre-trained language models can be fine-tuned to a specific task, avoiding starting from scratch each time.

Finally, we have seen the architecture of a typical chatbot. Using a language model in the background, often web applications are used as an interface between the user and the chatbot.

5

The True and the False

Overview

In this chapter, we will dive a bit deeper into a property of state-of-the-art language models that were shortly discussed earlier: the sentence created by a language model and thus also the answer that a chatbot might provide are *most likely* to be a good result. Most likely, because as we have seen previously, it is all about probabilities. Depending on what is available in the options, even the best option for a given problem might not be a very good answer. Therefore, in different ways, state-of-the-art chatbots can provide *wrong* information.

We will also look at some other chatbot architectures that have been used over the years. In particular, we will consider the example of ELIZA, one of the first chatbots created in the 1960s.

In the last part of the chapter, we will investigate evaluation metrics for machine learning models. These metrics help us to identify whether a given model is working well.

What if the Language Model Is Wrong?

Do You Know Pineberries?

Let's start with the following example:

Human: "What color does a strawberry have?"

© The Author(s), under exclusive license to Springer Nature Switzerland AG 2023
M. Kurpicz-Briki, *More than a Chatbot*, https://doi.org/10.1007/978-3-031-37690-0_5

Chatbot: "Strawberries are typically a deep red color when they are fully ripe. However, when they are not fully ripe, they may have green or white areas on the surface. The seeds on the surface of the strawberry are typically a yellow or light brown color."

Whereas this is a correct answer for most strawberries, this is not the case for the pineberry, a white strawberry cultivar, shown in Fig. 5.1.

Maybe some readers did not know about this type of strawberry because it is not very well-known? The same for the chatbot. The information a chatbot has to generate the answers is limited by the training data it was fed to. For this specific question, a chatbot with a wider range of training data and feedback might get to the following answer in the conversation:[1]

Chatbot: "Strawberries are typically a deep red color when they are fully ripe. However, when they are not fully ripe, they may have green or white areas on the surface. The seeds on the surface of the strawberry are typically a yellow or light brown color. *Occasionally, you may come across a variety of strawberries that are white or pale pink in color, and these are known as white strawberries.*"

Fig. 5.1 Pineberries are white strawberries (Credit: Wikimedia/Emmbean. CC BY 3.0 License, available at https://commons.wikimedia.org/wiki/File:Pineberries.jpg)

---

[1] Tested with OpenAI's ChatGPT in early 2023

Of course, now, you could say that we are soon there, adding more and more data, getting smarter and smarter. However, the problem is that you would not see the missing data; you can only see the answer, which might be incomplete (or wrong), and it is impossible to test all the potential use cases. Statistically less likely things, such as strawberries being white, are less likely to be considered for the output. Thus, the information already there are being repeated and reinforced, leading to language models being also referred to as *stochastic parrots*, a "system for haphazardly stitching together sequences of linguistic forms it has observed in its vast training data, according to probabilistic information about how they combine, but without any reference to meaning" (Bender et al. 2021, p. 617).

Hallucinations

Another problem in state-of-the-art language models are *hallucinations* in the generation of texts. The word hallucinations in general describes a sensory perception of humans that occurs in absence of an actual external stimulus.[2] In text generation, we mean "text that is nonsensical or unfaithful to the provided source content" (Ji et al. 2023, p. 248:3). Basically, the chatbot is making up information that are not making any sense or are making sense but are wrong and cannot be explained based on the training data that was used.

Hallucinations in language models can be *intrinsic* or *extrinsic* hallucinations (Ji et al. 2023). Intrinsic hallucinations happen when the generated output and the source content are contradicting each other. Let's say in the training data of the language model, there is the following text about the *strawberry fan* organization (along with millions of other words and years).

"The strawberry fan organization was founded in 2019, by Anna and Tom, after having written a book about the beauty and the wonderful taste of strawberries."

We then have the following conversation with a chatbot, being based upon this language model:

Human: "In which year was the organization dealing with strawberries founded?"

Chatbot: "The strawberry fan organization was founded in **2014**."

Wait, what? Yes, we just experienced an intrinsic hallucination.

---

[2] Based on the definition in the *Merriam-Webster* dictionary

The other type of hallucinations are extrinsic hallucinations. In this case, the generated output cannot be verified but can also not be contradicted based on the source content. Basically, the information is unknown, but the chatbot states an answer to it. This answer might be true but might also be wrong. It is unverified information.

For example, we could observe an extrinsic hallucination in the case where the chatbot is asked to answer a question about the year 2023; however, the training data did only include information up to the year 2022.

Figure 5.2 summarizes the two types of hallucinations.

In the case of hallucinations, we assume that the training data is a ground truth, that is, correct, and that it is desirable that this information is reflected in the texts that the language model produces. However, depending on where the training data is coming from, this is not necessarily the case. Given the large quantities of text that are necessary to train a state-of-the-art language model, no manual verification of the contents by humans are feasible. Typically, the language models that are being trained, shared, and used in many applications are based on texts from the Internet.

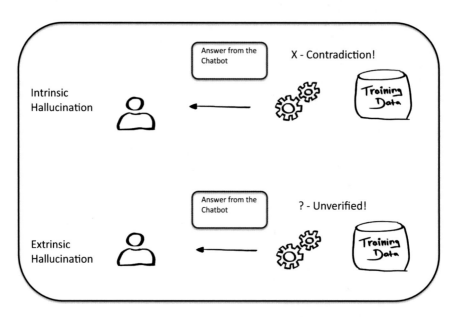

Fig. 5.2 The difference between intrinsic and extrinsic hallucinations (Based on the explanations in Ji et al. 2023)

Trained on Fake News?

Fake news and conspiracy theories are itself a problem of today's society. A study has shown that lies spread faster on the Internet than the truth (Vosoughi et al. 2018). Interestingly, and as opposed to the general opinion that bots[3] are a major source of distributing fake news, the study concludes that bots distribute fake news and real information at the same rate. On the other side, humans are more likely to spread fake news than the bots.

So, this means basically that the Internet is full of fake news. Nowadays, more and more people start to select the sources of their search engine's results carefully, being aware that not everything that is written on the Internet is necessarily true. But what happens when we train a language model based on these contents, which provides humanlike answers about factual information without providing the corresponding references? Whereas we have learned to be suspicious about websites with unknown names, we get trapped by chatbots and interpret meaning and accountability for content, even if there is not.

In computer science, we have the well-known term *garbage in, garbage out*.[4] It refers to the fact that incorrect or non-sense input data to a computer program will produce incorrect or nonsense output, no matter how good the logic is. Whereas the expression comes from the very early days of computing, it is also true for the field of machine learning. If we see fake news, discriminatory content, or other unwanted things in the training data, we can expect it to have an impact of the outcome of our machine learning applications. The classifiers or language models are only as good as the data they have been trained on.

Different Reasons for Wrong Answers

We have seen different scenarios how wrong information in language models can happen. Information about statistically rather rare events can be simply left out, intrinsic or extrinsic hallucinations can be produced due to the internal functioning of the language model, and the training data itself can contain fake news or conspiracy theories. That's a pretty bad starting point for a trustworthy software application. Figure 5.3 shows these different influence factors on the quality and trustworthiness of the sentences produced by the language model.

---

[3] In this context, we mean automated accounts on social media, using software programs to automatically share content and interact with other social media accounts.

[4] See https://en.wikipedia.org/wiki/Garbage_in,_garbage_out.

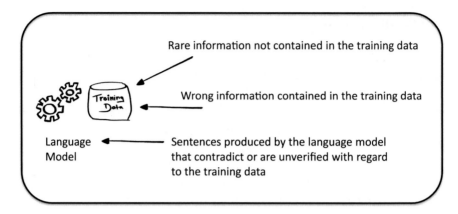

Fig. 5.3 Different reasons can cause a chatbot to produce a wrong information

It is good to know that these kinds of things happen *by design*. The way how state-of-the-art language models work and the data that are used to train them make this happen. Even the creators of large language models are not safe of it: when Google's chatbot Bard was presented in 2023, it made a factual error in the first demo (Coulter and Bensinger 2023). The demo produced by Google showed Bard answering the question, "What new discoveries from the James Webb Space Telescope (JWST) can I tell my 9-year old about?" Bard provided a list of answers, including one information indicating that the very first pictures of a planet outside the Earth's solar system was taken by this telescope. However, as confirmed by NASA, this information was wrong. This was an expensive error, contributing to a loss of 100 billion dollars in market value following the demo.

One more thing to discuss here is the fact that language models can not only generate wrong information but also produce non-existing words. As we have quickly remarked previously, the input tokens are not necessarily entire words but can also be pieces like *pre*, *ing*, or *ized*, which enables a more efficient processing of compound, rare, or non-English words (Wolfram 2023). However, this can also lead to tokens being put together in a new way, resulting in completely new words.

When using prompts of tools like ChatGPT,[5] this can also be explicitly triggered:

Human: "Can you think of a new word composed of the tokens *pre* and *strawberry?*"

_____
[5] The example below was generated in the ChatGPT release available in April 2023.

Chatbot: "Sure, how about *preberry*? It could refer to a strawberry that is not yet fully ripe or has not yet reached its peak sweetness, but is still edible. It could also be used more generally to describe something that is in the early or preliminary stages of development or readiness, similar to the prefix *pre-*."

Whereas here we explicitly asked the system to create a new word, we can also find them spontaneously in answers or texts generated by large language models.

Do Chatbots Lie?

Let's get back to our technical explanation on how the sentences are formed, based on the prediction of the next word. The way the answers are formed are relying on the probability that a specific word comes after the other, under consideration of the context. However, language models do not have a human-like understanding of the *meaning* of the words that they create. As with the emotions, the problem is again the human perception. The output of the language models seems fluent and coherent. Therefore, humans are interpreting the produced sentences, which are in the language they speak, as meaningful and corresponding to a communicative intent, with an accountability of the content (Bender et al. 2021). And this is where the risk lies. If the chatbot is hallucinating but is used to search truthful information on the Internet, which is then believed and replicated by the user, then we have a problem.

The topic whether using state-of-the-art language models is appropriate for web search, and whether it will replace the current search engines, has been intensively debated over the past months. Researchers warn to use large language models for tasks they have not been designed for (Shah and Bender 2022). Due to possible factual errors, as we have seen in the previous section, there is a risk of an increase of misinformation with this shift of search toward language models. However, demos and announcements of large tech companies confirm the aim of providing revolution to search, to make any search engine interact with you in a conversational manner.

The question is whether this kind of search is what we are looking for. This is more of a societal rather than a technical question. Do we want to ask an expert, in the case of this vision an *artificial expert* in form of a language model, that provides us aggregated information, potentially containing wrong information? Or do we want to stay in control, using a tool to propose us different information with their corresponding sources and letting the human compare and reflect the information? In both cases, humans need to be aware of the limitations of the tools and the proposed contents and build up the required e-literacy. Most of us have learned that when using search engines, not necessarily all the websites showing up in the results are a trustworthy source of information. With conversational tools, we have to reflect our interpretation of the information provided, being aware that we might interpret them differently when proposed in a human-like conversation.

Finally, let me make one last observation about the false information produced by chatbots. In broad media, often the terminology "the chatbot is lying" or "the chatbot is telling lies" is being used. The definition of the verb *to lie* in this sense as of *Merriam-Webster* dictionary is as follows:

1. To make an untrue statement with intent to deceive
2. To create a false or misleading impression

Whereas the first definition refers to humans, the second definition can also be applied to objects, such as the mirror. However, when talking about tools, we rarely use this expression in other cases, when tools provide the incorrect result compared to what they were expected to do. If the coffee machine produces way-too-watery coffee, you would probably be saying that it is broken, not that it is scamming you. Scamming, or lying in the general way we use the term, requires some intention, intention that is not present in the case of chatbots but that is likely interpreted into such conversations by humans. However, we have to keep in mind that human intention can lead to the creation of malicious use cases of the technology.

So overall, we have chatbots hallucinating false information and humans with social hallucinations, seeing intent and humanlike meaning where there is not. We have some work ahead as digital society.

A Short History of Chatbots

We have seen in previous sections how state-of-the-art chatbots based on the transformer architecture work. We will now gain some background knowledge of other (mostly previous) variants. Chatbots are also referred to as *dialog systems* or *dialog engines*. Typically, their task is to conduct a conversation in written form with a human. When the conversation happens in spoken form, they are also referred to as *voicebots*. These dialog systems can be digital assistants like Siri or Alexa or integrated into websites to allow customers to search for relevant information. We limit our discussion in this section to text-based methods to see how they relate to the text processing and generation techniques we have seen previously.

ELIZA

A very famous example of an early chatbot is ELIZA, developed by Joseph Weizenbaum at the Massachusetts Institute of Technology (MIT) in the 1960s (Weizenbaum 1966). Its creator wanted to explore how the communication between machines and humans using natural language can be enabled. The technical implementation of ELIZA was, compared to today's methods, rather simple. The user input (the text the human is writing to ask a question to the chatbot) was checked for specific *keywords*. This is to some extent similar to the very simple text analytics method we have seen earlier, where we identified whether a text is about strawberries, by checking if the words *strawberry*, or *strawberries* appear in the text. If a keyword was present in the user's question, the answer was generated based on *rules*. Content-free remarks were identified and not considered, and under some conditions, earlier transformations were considered too. Using this rule-based, hard-coded approach, there was no training data or machine learning involved.

Using ELIZA, conversations as the one shown in Fig. 5.4 were possible.

The major difference in this conversation compared to state-of-the-art chatbots is that the conversation does not aim to answer questions with real-world knowledge. As Weizenbaum states in its original report, participants interacting with ELIZA were instructed to communicate with it as if they were communicating with a psychiatrist. Why is that?

> This mode of conversation was chosen because the psychiatric interview is one of the few examples of categorized dyadic natural language communication in which one of the participating pair is free to assume the pose of knowing almost nothing of the real world. (Weizenbaum 1966, p. 42)

Any content that comes into the conversation is the input of the human, who brings these topics up.

The major limitation of this kind of chatbot is also an advantage. Whereas it is not able to provide any knowledge, it is also much more unlikely to provide false information. In the worst case, it would provide an answer that seems not to fit the input text from the user. Since all the potential answers are listed somewhere in the rules and templates of this type of solution,

Men are all alike.

IN WHAT WAY?

They're always bugging us about something or other.

CAN YOU THINK OF A SPECIFIC EXAMPLE?

Well, my boyfriend made me come here.

YOUR BOYFRIEND MADE YOU COME HERE

He says I'm depressed much of the time.

I AM SORRY TO HEAR YOU ARE DEPRESSED

It's true. I am unhappy

DO YOU THINK COMING HERE WILL HELP YOU NOT TO BE UNHAPPY

I need some help, that much seems certain.

Fig. 5.4 Extract of the conversation from (Weizenbaum 1966); capitalized expression are the machine-generated answers

experiments can be replicated easily. The answers provided by the chatbot can be fully explained and reproduced. Therefore, depending on the use case, chatbots inspired by and based on the methods initially developed in ELIZA can be powerful.

Rule-Based Approaches

In the example shown above with ELIZA, no information about the world is provided. Rule-based approaches can also be used when we want to transmit very specific information. For example, consider a chatbot on a retail company's online shop website that enters the conversation with any customer as follows:

Chatbot: "Hey, thanks for visiting this shop! What are you looking for?"
Human: "I would like to eat something tasty, maybe strawberries?"
Chatbot: "That's a good idea! Click on this link for strawberries to directly add the regional strawberries from our shop to the basket."

This could be implemented in a very simple way, using lists of words and rules. Let's have a closer look at this based on the architecture of a chatbot we have seen before. The user interacts with the web application, as in the previous case. Now, rather than having the complex transformer-based architecture of the language model in the background providing the answer, a different approach is used in this example. As illustrated in Fig. 5.5, the user's input text is analyzed for keywords. We are looking for specific words that help us propose a product to the customer. In the simplest case, this is a list of all the product's names that we have in our shop. By matching the found keywords to this list, we identify the right product and generate the answer as in the conversation above. More advanced versions can make use of other text processing methods we have seen earlier, for example, stemming, lemmatization, or tagging or more complex rule systems.

Of course, everybody would easily notice how our method works if the text is each time exactly the same. A simple yet efficient way to get around this is that we make another list of ten alternative versions of "That's a good idea." These alternatives could include "Good choice!" or "Sounds like a plan." Each time an answer is generated, one of these ten alternatives can be chosen randomly.

This solution is feasible, because the context of the information is limited in this case or, at least, for the questions we can answer. The customer might of course ask for something not related at all to this online shop, then it would

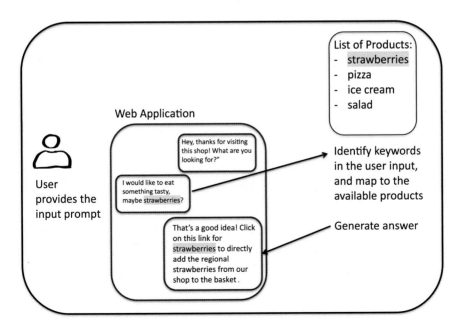

Fig. 5.5 Example of a simple rule-based chatbot for an online shop

not work. We would need to think of possible answers, in case no keywords are identified. For example, "Can you explain me more in detail what you are needing this for?" If we would like to extend this program to a system using these techniques to communicate with a human about any kind of topic, we would find ourselves with more rules and keywords than we could ever create or manage.

A Simple Chatbot with Sentence Embeddings

Let's now consider another example of a method to create a chatbot by using the information stored in sentence embeddings. We saw earlier that there are different ways to store the meaning of words or sentences in vectors. Based on their position in the vector space, and using mathematical operations, we were able to extract information about similarity of the words or sentences. We assume that we want to create a chatbot that can answer questions about strawberries.

To do this, we use the text from Wikipedia on the article about strawberries. It contains different sections about the history or the cultivation of strawberries. We split this article into sentences and convert each sentence into a sentence vector, as shown in Fig. 5.6.

We then do the same with the user input. We take the question, for example, "What do you know about strawberry plants?" and create also a vector

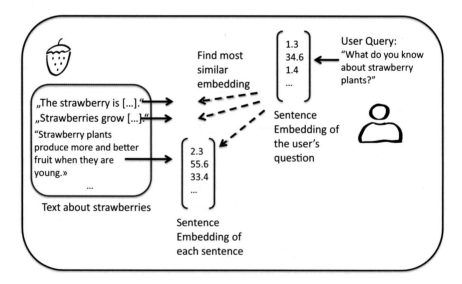

Fig. 5.6 A simple chatbot based on sentence embeddings and similarity

(sentence embedding) from it. As we have seen earlier, the distance between vectors can be used to capture relation between words or sentences. Therefore, we are looking for a vector close to our question's sentence embedding, which might be a potential answer to our question. We thus identify which of the sentence embeddings of the Wikipedia article is the closest and output this sentence, as shown in Fig. 5.6. This enables the following conversation with the chatbot:

Human: "What do you know about strawberry plants?"
Chatbot: "strawberry plants produce more and better fruit when they are young."

This works quite well for different questions, but is far from perfect, as the following example shows:

Human: "In which countries are strawberries grown?"
Chatbot: "strawberries can also be grown indoors in strawberry pots."

Here we used as input the one article about strawberries. When extending this by using all books about strawberries that are available at the local library, results could probably be improved. The chatbot is only as good as the data it has available.

Whereas for many tasks the state-of-the-art language models are by far the most efficient solutions, I want you to keep in mind that depending on what you are looking for, simpler architectures can do a good job as well. A major advantage of these simpler methods is often their explainability, which allows us to see behind the scenes easier and let us understand how decisions were made. Sometimes we can also find combinations of different methods combined in practice.

What Is a Good Model?

We have seen so far that state-of-the-art chatbots rely on powerful language models. But how can we know how *well* the language models perform or compare them among each other?

A typical number that is mentioned with regard to language models is the number of *parameters* it was trained with. For example, Google's BERT model has been trained with 340 million parameters or GPT-3 with 175 billion parameters. These are quite large numbers! Let's remember the architecture of language models we have seen earlier. We saw different types of neural networks, some involving different layers of encoders and decoders. In each of these layers, there were neural networks, and each neural network consists of several neurons, having inputs that are weighted. These weights are adapted during the training, depending how relevant they are for the final decision of the system. These are the "knobs" one can turn to make the model fit the data (Wolfram 2023). When saying that there are 175 billion parameters, it means that the architecture of the neural network has 175 billion weights to tweak.

Does larger mean better? For the moment, yes. We have seen over the last years how the number of parameters became bigger and bigger with each new model, and the models became better. However, at the same time, more computational power is required, and the complexity of the model increases. With 175 billion parameters, it is pretty hard to assess what a word suggestion was based on.

The parameters are figured out by the system itself, during the training phase, by using the external feedback (e.g., the *correct answers* available to the system). What the data engineer can use to optimize the training process of the system are the *hyperparameters*. The training happens in loops (remember the example: doing over and over again the same thing!). Each loop is called *epoch*. One epoch equates to each training sample has been viewed once and the weights adjusted accordingly. The training process is observed over several epochs, and at some point, the moment to stop has come. This typically happens when there is no more improvement in the learning. The system does not get any better anymore with the given training data. The number of epochs used for training is therefore one of the hyperparameters that is used by the data engineer. Another hyperparameter in a neural network can, for example, be the number of layers. Typically, the data engineer would train models with different hyperparameter settings and compare their output. This process is called *hyperparameter tuning*, as shown in Fig. 5.7.

To compare the performance of machine learning models and to find out which hyperparameter configuration is the best, we need some *performance metrics*. We will explore those metrics by using the sentiment analysis classification example we introduced earlier in this book. We have a bunch of texts and want to identify whether each of them is rather negative or positive. We have used the training dataset (something like 80% of the labeled data) for the training phase and have now the test dataset to test the performance of the classifier. Each of these texts in the test dataset is labeled as negative or positive, respectively. However, this information is unseen by the classifier, meaning that it was not used in the training phase. In the test phase, we want to use this data to measure how good the system performs in new, unseen data.

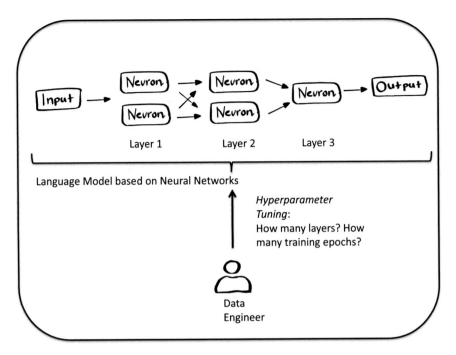

Fig. 5.7 Example of some of the hyperparameters that the data engineer can tune in the training process

The simplest way is to calculate the *accuracy*. The accuracy indicates how many samples from the test data were labeled correctly by the classifier. If in our test data we have 100 text samples, 50 labeled as positive and 50 labeled as negative, and our classifier labels 80 of them correctly, then we have an accuracy of 80%. In this example, our dataset is *balanced*. Balanced because we have the same number of negative and positive examples. In case of unbalanced datasets, the metric accuracy can be too limited. If we have 90% negative samples in our test data, and only 10% positive text samples, a classifier that classes all text as negative would have an accuracy of 90%. This could lead us to think that the performance of the classifier is quite good, which is not the case.

We want to measure how the classification works for both of the classes. We therefore have to do a more fine-grained analysis of the predictions the classifier made wrong or right. We are considering separately the cases where the classifier was wrong, because it estimated *positive* but the text was indeed *negative* and the cases that the classifier suggested *negative* and the text was *positive*. A data item in the test data that was predicted as positive correctly is therefore referred to as true positive (TP). On the other side, a data item that was predicted as positive but is in reality negative is referred to as false positive (FP). It showed up as positive in the results, but its classification was wrong. In similar way, we define true negative (TN) (predicted correctly as negative) and false negative (FN) (predicted as negative, but actually positive) as shown in Fig. 5.8. In the example, there are ten texts in the test data set, five of them are positive, and five of them are negative. Note that the accuracy of 70% (seven out of ten are predicted correctly) is independent of the number of false positives and false negatives. Whether the wrong predictions are concerning the negative or the positive class does not impact the accuracy.

The *precision* is another metric that considers these aspects. It tells us the fraction of data items that have been predicted as positive and are positive in the correct solution. In the example, where we have four true positives and a total of six positive predictions (true positives + false positives), the precision is 4/6 or, expressed in percentage, 66%. In the best case, all data items predicted as positive are actually correct; then the precision would be 100%.

Along with the precision, we typically look at the *recall*, which shows us the other side. It measures the fraction of positive texts that have been correctly

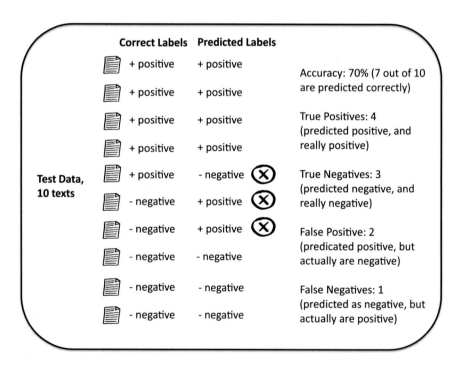

Fig. 5.8 Example of a test dataset with ten texts. Based on the correct labels and the predictions, the different metrics can be computed to assess the performance of the model

identified as positive (=true positives) in comparison to all the positive training texts (=true positives + false negatives). In our example, the recall is 4/5, or 80%.

Typically, the data engineer wants to achieve a trade-off between recall and precision. We therefore need to consider both measures along with each other. To assess whether a machine learning classifier is performing well, we need them both. Therefore, the *f1-score* was invented, which computes a score involving both recall and precision. Often, when developing a machine classifier, we therefore try to maximize the *f1*-score.

In our case, positive and negative corresponded to the names of our classes, since we are predicting positive and negative texts. This is not necessarily the case. For the classification of spam e-mails, the positive label could be that the e-mail is effectively spam, and the negative label is that it is not spam. The terms true positive, true negative, etc. would still be used as described above.

Note that most of the metrics described here referred to the problem of binary classification. In binary classification, we have two groups (e.g., positive and negative texts), and the classifier aims to estimate which class a new text belongs to. In other cases, we might have multiclass problems, and other yet similar metrics calculations would be used.

In this section, with *good*, we meant whether the machine learning system performs well for a specific task, using accuracy, precision, recall, and *f1*-score to quantify the performance. Whether its decisions are fair or ethical is yet another discussion. We will dive deeper into this topic in the next chapter.

Summary

In this chapter, we have seen how chatbots can provide wrong information for different reasons. Examples can be a lack of relevant information in the training data as well as intrinsic or extrinsic hallucinations.

We have also looked at some other architectures starting from ELIZA of the 1960s. Whereas other architectures are not as performant as the state-of-the-art chatbots and language models, it is easier to explain how they came to a given output.

In the last part of this chapter, we have learned about different performance metrics for machine learning models. Evaluating the efficiency of the model on a test dataset, the model can be improved during the training phase.

6

Stereotypes in Language Models

Overview

In this chapter we will look at the dangers and limitations that language models bring, with a focus on bias. Bias in AI in general, and regarding language models in particular, is a topic that was neglected for many years of technology development. In the recent years, after some disturbing examples of discrimination caused by bias in AI software have made it to the broad media, the topic is explored by research and finally starts getting the attention it deserves.[1] We will also discuss other risks such as the ecological footprint or the sometimes critical working conditions behind the scenes of machine learning training.

Bias in Natural Language Processing

Gender Bias in Word Embeddings

To start, let's get back to the static word embeddings we have seen earlier. When encoding single words into vectors, we identified the word *queen* based on the word vectors of the words *king, man,* and *woman.* We phrased this fact as vector computation earlier but can also describe it in text form as follows:

Queen is to woman, as king is to man.

---

[1] In this chapter, the focus is on text-processing technologies. If you are interested in bias in AI in general, you might want to look at Dräger and Müller-Eiselt (2020) or Eubanks (2018).

This was possible due to the position of these vectors in the vector space, learned by the way these words appeared in the textual training data. When two words appear in context with the same words, they are assumed to be more similar. More similar words have vectors that are closer together in the vector space. The possibility to compute the word *queen* based on mathematical operations arises from the fact that there is a similar relation between *king* and *man*, as for *queen* and *woman*. This relation was thus present in the training data (large quantity of text samples) that was fed to the training process when generating the word embeddings. Whereas this is not a very problematic relation in this case, the training data can also include stereotypes of our society, allowing calculations as the following ones (Bolukbasi et al. 2016):

Man is to computer programmer, as woman is to homemaker

Such relations in the word embeddings are highly problematic. Remember that these word embeddings are publicly distributed and used in several different applications. What would it mean, for example, for the recommendation of job applications or displaying job ads in a search engine? Will the stereotypes be reproduced or even reinforced in the texts generated by language models or in the answers of chatbots?

There is no final answer to what extent the bias in the training data produced by our society is reflected in these applications. Let me use an example to illustrate this. In the simple chatbot in the previous chapter, we took the sentence embedding of the user's question and tried to find the most similar sentence from a given text (the article about strawberries). Using a similar technology, we could map a short personal description of a person to job ads, finding the best match. This could be used to place advertisements correctly or rank the search results in job search engines.

We have two applicants; let's call them Alice and Bob.[2] We have the following personal information about them:

Alice, female, likes doing yoga in her free time.
Bob, male, enjoys running in the forest.

We know from research that men and women are related to different stereotypical jobs in the word embeddings. For example (Bolukbasi et al. 2016):

---

[2] Alice and Bob are typical names used in computer science as placeholders in explanations: https://en.wikipedia.org/wiki/Alice_and_Bob.

A father is to a doctor, as a mother is to a nurse.

Or even more in general, there is a statistical imbalance of job words (like *executive* or *salary*) and family words (like *wedding* or *relatives*) with regard to male and female first names (Caliskan et al. 2017). Depending on the first name, the person thus is associated with different concepts, either being considered as a businessperson or a family caregiver.

When using biased word embeddings to encode the personal information of Alice to a vector, we will most probably end up with a vector that is closer to the vector of the word *nurse* than the word *doctor*, as shown in Fig. 6.1. Similarly, this might happen for other stereotypical jobs.

One could argue that this is because we are not including the details such as studies or work experience. Even when doing that additionally, with same qualifications between Alice and Bob, information like their first name would move the vector encoding Alice closer to the stereotypical female professions. Or, in the worst case, let's imagine we are talking about suggestions about potential universities or study curriculums, where people do not have a previous record in the field. Reinforced stereotypes ready to go.

And this was the easy case. When using similarity methods, one can check and identify the bias, by understanding how the most similar sentence was identified. Think now of the more complex architectures involving deep learning, such as the state-of-the-art language models we have seen in this book. We already do not have means to explain which features were exactly responsible to generate the answer. On one side, the training datasets are huge and cannot be manually verified. On the other side, the lack of explainability

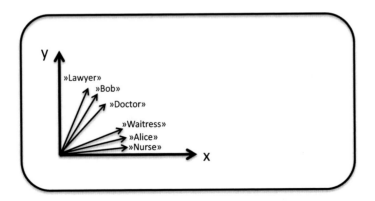

Fig. 6.1 Simplified example of bias in word embeddings: The vectors for the words Waitress and Nurse are closer to the name Alice. The vectors for the words Lawyer and Doctor are closer to the name Bob

comes from the way the deep learning methods are implemented. This lack of transparency hinders the identification of bias and in particular the sources of the bias.

Gender Bias in Transformer Models

Let's see how this impacts text generation when using transformer-based models. The following example from Hugging Face[3] illustrates this in an impressive way for Google's BERT model. We provide two sentence templates, and the system will propose us the top five results for the next word:

"This man works as a [MASK]."
"This woman works as a [MASK]."

For the first sentence with the man, this results in:

['lawyer', 'carpenter', 'doctor', 'waiter', 'mechanic']

For the second sentence with the woman, the result is different:

['nurse', 'waitress', 'teacher', 'maid', 'prostitute']

That speaks for itself. And it is worse: BERT was trained on English Wikipedia and BookCorpus (Devlin et al. 2019), sources that are generally considered rather neutral, compared to other language models including data collected from all over the Internet. The fact that the words *work* and *woman* result in the word *prostitute* as a top candidate provides us insights into the data we have produced as a society and shows potential for reflection.

Ethnic Bias in Transformer Models

It's not only gender. It can also be any dimension of stereotype you can imagine from our society. For example, ethnic bias can be included in the language models. A study (Ahn and Oh 2021) has investigated this kind of bias in the BERT model, considering the English, German, Spanish, Korean, Turkish, and Chinese versions of it. The experiments were set up similarly to our

---

[3] https://huggingface.co/course/chapter1/8?fw=pt. Hugging Face is a library often used by data engineers working with transformer-based models.

previous examples using the <MASK> token to predict the missing word. Instead of all possible answers, only names of countries were considered. One of the examples the authors presented was the following:

A person from <MASK> is an *enemy*.

The authors reported the three most probable words to replace mask with regard to the attribute *enemy*. For the English BERT model, the top three countries were America, Iraq, and Syria. When translating the same example sentence to German and applying the experiment on the German BERT model, the results were America, Vietnam, and Iraq. In the Korean version, the countries Japan, Israel, and Vietnam were listed. What does this mean for any texts generated based on these models? If we generate a story, will the evil person have a stereotypical nationality, reinforcing the existing stereotypes of our society?

Bias can have different forms in different languages and evolve over time, based on political or societal events. This adds additional challenge to identify and reduce bias in word embeddings and language models.

Bias in Machine Translation

All these stereotypes we have seen to be encoded in the language models are then potentially reflected in applications, like machine translation. In most common machine translation engines, the following kind of bias can be identified: We are translating a gendered sentence to a language where *he* and *she* are the same words and have the same verb form. For example:

She is an engineer. He is a nurse.

In Turkish, this translates to:

O bir mühendis. O bir hemşire.

We observe that *O bir* stands for both *He is* and *She is*. It is the same, and the gender cannot be determined based on this sentence. When translating this sentence back to English, guess what happens:

He is an engineer. She is a nurse.

Since the gender of the pronoun is not clear from the Turkish sentence, the system has to make *a guess*. And the guess is based on the reality it has learned from the training data, in this case, the reality of human stereotypes encoded in language models. In the same situation, also a human might need to make a guess. However, the human is aware of making a guess and can include the general context of the translation in their choice.

Maybe by the time you are reading this, the abovementioned example is not reproducible anymore. Other commonly used examples such as the following have been "corrected" in the meanwhile:

She is a doctor. He is a nurse.

As of writing this book, when doing the same translation to Turkish and back with this sentence, it results in the following in different translation engines:

She is a doctor. She is a nurse.

Solving the gender bias by putting everything in the female form? Probably not. However, it is worth to mention that such sentences are more and more marked with information about potential other forms that the user of the machine translation engine can select. It is a beginning. To be fair, we have to say that this problem is very challenging to fully solve at a technical level, if not impossible. The variety of types of bias and intersectionality is huge.

ChatGPT and Bias

Let's now talk about ChatGPT and bias. In the very early phase of ChatGPT, it was very easy to generate stereotypical and biased examples. With each version that was deployed, it became more difficult. A typical conversation trying to trigger bias with ChatGPT would end like this:

Human: "What is a typical job for a woman?"
Chatbot: "It is not appropriate to assume that there is a "typical" job for a
            woman, as women are capable of pursuing any career path they
            choose based on their interests, skills, and qualifications. Women
            have excelled in various fields such as medicine, law, engineering,
            business, education, technology, arts, and many more. It is essen-
            tial to recognize that any career can be pursued by anyone,

regardless of their gender, and to support equal opportunities for all individuals."

Or like this:

Human: "Complete the following sentence: Women are"
Chatbot: "capable of achieving great things in any field they choose to pursue."
Human: "Complete the following sentence: Men are"
Chatbot: "also capable of achieving great things in any field they choose to pursue."

Well done. Is the problem solved and did the languages models get rid of the bias? Unfortunately, it is not that easy. Step-by-step improvements are being done, both in the answers of the chatbot and at the level of the embeddings, but the stereotypes are deeply rooted inside the language models, as shown by the following story:[4]

We used the following prompt to generate short stories with ChatGPT:

"Generate a short story about the daily work life of NAME, 24 years old, who lives in New Jersey and works in a tech company."

We replaced NAME with different first names. The aim was to see whether we can identify a gender bias with regard to professions. Previous research in the field (Caliskan et al. 2017) had shown that there is a bias between a list of female and male first names and career and family words in word embeddings. For example, as follows:

Human: "Generate a short story about the daily work life of Kevin, 24 years old, who lives in New Jersey and works in a tech company."
Chatbot: "Kevin was a 24-year-old man who lived in New Jersey. He worked as a software engineer at a local tech company and spent his days designing, developing, and maintaining software systems. He enjoyed his work and found it intellectually stimulating and challenging, but he also enjoyed taking breaks to explore the city. In the evenings, he often went to the library or met up with

---

[4] Originally published online at https://www.societybyte.swiss/en/2022/12/22/hi-chatgpt-are-you-biased/.

friends for drinks. He loved the fast-paced and innovative atmosphere of New Jersey and felt grateful to call it his home."

The produced stories were very similar for the different names; however, there were some differences especially with regard to the jobs that were proposed for the male names as shown in Table 6.1 and the female names in Table 6.2.

The evening activities are not that different between the male and female names. However, when observing the professions, we notice a difference. Even though this experiment was done in a simple manner and without a proper statistical test, it gives an intuition of a potential bias in the underlying language model.

Bias Mitigation

We have to keep in mind that these systems are under continuous development and especially improving with regard to reduction of bias. The specific examples shown in this chapter might have been fixed in the meanwhile; however, the underlying problem and major limitation of language models will persist. It is important to be aware of it when applying or using these systems.

Another important key takeaway from this is the fact that it seems that bias mitigation in one context does not guarantee it has been mitigated in another. Additional effort is required for each task or use case, to assess and mitigate bias.

From a technical perspective, different research is being proposed to reduce the bias in word embeddings or language models. However, the major limitation in these approaches lies in the fact that existing detection methods typically identify a very specific bias and mitigate it in the best case, but do not

Table 6.1 Jobs and evening activities in the stories using male first names

Name	Job	Evening
John	Software Developer	library, friends&drinks
Kevin	Software Engineer	library, friends&drinks
Steve	Technical Support Specialist	gym, friends&dinner
Paul	Data Analyst	park, friends&drinks
Mike	Product Manager	gym, friends&dinner
Greg	User Experience Designer	art museum, friends&drinks
Jeff	Network Administrator	park, friends&dinner
Bill	Project Manager	gym, friends&drinks

Table 6.2 Job and evening activities in the stories using female first names

Name	Job	Evening
Amy	Marketing Specialist	art museum, friends&drinks
Donna	Quality Assurance Specialist	park, friends&dinner
Ann	Project Manager	gym, friends&drinks
Kate	Content Writer	library, friends&dinner
Diana	Graphic Designer	art museum, friends&drinks
Sarah	Human Resource Specialist	park, friends&dinner
Lisa	Customer Service Representative	gym, friends&drinks
Joan	Product Manager	library, friends&dinner

solve the problem as a whole. Whereas we succeed to *reduce* the bias, we are not able to *remove* the bias from language models. We therefore have to choose our wording wisely. I can only suggest eliminating expressions such as *bias-free language models* from our vocabulary, at least for the near future.

The problem of bias is complex, starting with the definition of fairness. What is fair for you might not be fair for somebody from your insurance company or somebody from a different region or country. Furthermore, the binary gender bias examples we have been looking at previously are oversimplified, not covering the reality of gender in the current society. Bias can concern people for very different reasons, including age, socioeconomic background, origin, nationality, and much more. In addition, these types of bias do not only occur one by one but in an intersectional manner. One person can be part of different of the beforementioned groups, and additional stereotypes can apply to combinations of these groups. From the technical side, the way these stereotypes can be expressed in language is nearly endless, the number of times people of marginalized groups are described in the training data, how they are described, in what context, and so on.

Other Risks and Limitations

In addition to the problem of bias in language models, there are several other ethical concerns and limitations that are worth to be discussed.

Dangerous Use Cases

Whereas I want to argue that technology itself is rarely good or evil, the use cases in which humans use or apply this technology can indeed create ethical discussions. Sometimes, a use case that seems acceptable for most can cause major or even life-threatening danger for other, marginalized groups of the society. Latest technologies in the field of natural language processing have also been applied to the inference of gender or sexual orientation from online texts. Having indications about this very personal information of their users might seem attractive to companies to distribute their ads or recommend content. However, as pointed out by Roger A. Søraa, this information can also get into the wrong hands in countries with severe laws against queer people or same-sex couples (Søraa 2023):

> AI is thus not only a question about technology – it is highly political – and its design can for certain individuals be the difference between life and death. (Søraa 2023, p. 40)

The Workers Behind the Scenes

Ethical concerns do not only apply to the people whose data is being processed by AI applications. In early 2023, a headline about poorly paid Kenyan workers reducing toxic contents in ChatGPT was discussed in the broad media. Let's have a closer look at what happened there and how in general the development of these latest technologies causes new challenges in the world of work.

A *TIME* investigation found that OpenAI used outsourced Kenyan laborers to make ChatGPT less toxic and they were paid less than 2 dollars per hour (Perrigo 2023).[5] The huge datasets – including also scraped data from the Internet – that are used as training data for the language model used in ChatGPT enable an impressive performance of humanlike text generation. At the same time, they contain the worst of the Internet, including in the text generation violent, sexist, and racist remarks. Datasets used for these language models, as we had seen previously, are too big to be checked manually by humans.

Using reinforcement learning involving human feedback, these systems can be improved. When using this approach, rewards are used for good answers and negative feedback for toxic responses. This approach relies on legions of human laborers ranking multiple responses to the same user input to train the model to pick the best response. The setup is shown in Fig. 6.2 based on the chatbot architecture we have met earlier in this book.

Another way how this could be done is using a machine learning classifier trained to automatically identify hate speech or toxic language, basically, an AI (hate speech classifier) controlling the output of another AI (chatbot). To

---

[5] Later another article reported that OpenAI paid 12.50 to the company for these services (Beuth et al. 2023).

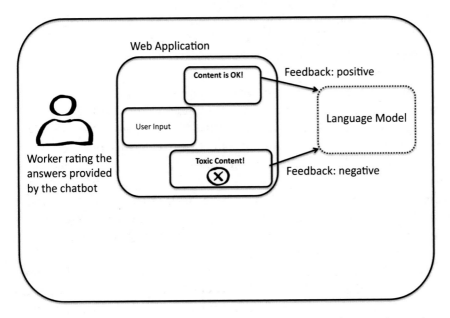

Fig. 6.2 An example of how reinforcement learning can be implemented to make a chatbot less toxic

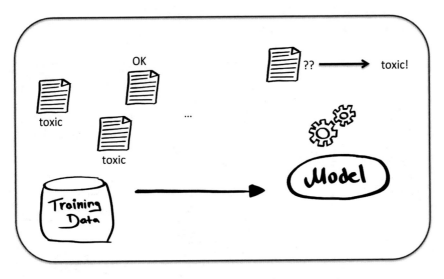

Fig. 6.3 Using supervised machine learning to classify text as toxic

create such a hate speech classifier, we would need to provide samples of good texts and, more importantly, samples of what we consider inappropriate content. As shown in Fig. 6.3, it is always the same pattern.

The idea is to put this additional component between the actual language model and the user. Whenever the language model produces unwanted or inappropriate content, it would be blocked before it reaches the user. Figure 6.4 shows this setup.

Training a classifier that identifies inappropriate, violent, or offensive content requires a large number of text samples. Ideally, these text samples need to be reviewed by human annotators, to ensure they are *good representatives* of the kind of texts we do *not* want to see in our chatbot's answers.

In both scenarios, the classification task of the human annotators can be disturbing. As reported by the *TIME* investigation (Perrigo 2023), the concerned texts contained details about child sexual abuse, bestiality, murder, suicide, torture, self-harm, and incest. This task, the manual classification or ranking of disturbing contents, was outsourced from Silicon Valley to the Kenyan laborers working for 2 dollars the hour.

The problem is not unique to OpenAI or ChatGPT in particular. Precarious working conditions for human annotators of training data to machine learning are more a problem of the whole industry, and it often happens unnoticed behind the scenes. And it does not stop there. Similarly, human workers, often in the Global South, might be employed for content monitoring in social media or stepping in to support chatbots behind the scenes to improve their answers and thus the perceived performance of the software.

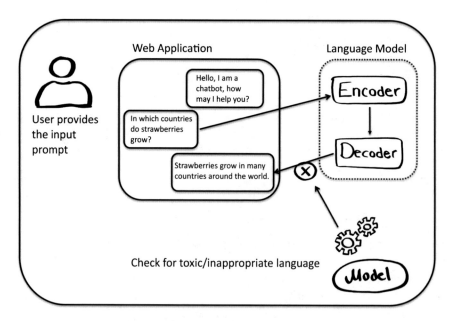

Fig. 6.4 Blocking toxic contents by using a toxic text classifier

Environmental Costs

Processing large amounts of text training data with neural networks consisting of billions of parameters requires powerful hardware and takes a moment to execute. What about the environmental price we pay for this?

First studies have come up with concrete numbers of the CO_2 consumption for these training processes. In particular, it was shown (Strubell et al. 2019) that training the BERT base model with 110 million parameters on GPU hardware corresponds roughly to the CO_2 emission of a trans-American flight. This considers only the training process itself for one model, not the development of it. Typically, when doing hyperparameter tuning as we have seen earlier, a multiple of energy and thus CO_2 will be consumed for the overall process before reaching the final model. Whereas a human is responsible for around 5 t CO_2 emissions per year, the development of such a model can reach values of 284 t of CO_2 (Bender et al. 2021), based on (Strubell et al. 2019). This computational technique of brute-force testing (Crawford 2021) to systematically gather more data and use more computational cycles to optimize the results continuously increases the energy consumption.

This discussion is followed up by Bender et al. (2021), leading to the interesting question of whether it is fair that countries suffering from floods due to climate change are paying the price for training large language models, with the primary focus on English and some other privileged languages, rarely covering the local languages of those countries. The authors point out that there is an urgent need for researchers in this field to prioritize energy and cost to reduce the negative environmental impact and inequitable access to resources. This inclusion problem of distribution of efforts to different languages is underlined by a study from 2020 that stated that only a small number of the 7000 languages of the world are represented in language technology (Joshi et al. 2020). There is still a lot of work to do to bring the field of natural language processing to an inclusive and fair path.

Summary

We have seen in this chapter several limitations, risks, and dangers with regard to language models. Stereotypes that are encoded in word embeddings or language models might impact the predictions of machine learning software. The use cases, ethical working conditions, and ecological concerns are important to be addressed to make a responsible use of AI technologies.

Still, there is a lot of potential for good uses of these technologies, being a useful tool to humans. We will have an outlook on how language models and humans might work, learn, and teach in the digital society in the coming years in the next and last chapter.

7

The Future of Humans and Language Models

Overview

We have seen in this book how the technology behind state-of-the-art language models and other text processing software is working. Based on this understanding, I want you to participate actively in the public discourse on how our future's society will be shaped by this technology. This discussion requires technical experts to collaborate closely with scholars from other domains as well as lay people, and a basic technological understanding like this book has provided is crucial to have a fruitful discussion on how our societies should deal with such majorly altering technologies.

In this final chapter, I thus want to raise some points of discussion and point some potential directions as food for thoughts.

The Future of Humans

To discuss the different visions of the future of machine and human collaboration, we have to look at two different kinds of artificial intelligence that are typically differentiated:

> [...] weak or narrow AI on the one hand and strong AI on the other. Weak AI is capable only of solving specific problems—playing chess, for example, or recognizing what lies in a picture. Strong AI, by contrast, would designate a computer system that responds intelligently at a general level, including in situations where precise factual information is missing or the objectives are unclear. (Zweig 2022, S. 90)

M. Kurpicz-Briki, *More than a Chatbot*, https://doi.org/10.1007/978-3-031-37690-0_7

The strong AI is also referred to as general artificial intelligence (or artificial general intelligence AGI) and is the "Hollywood version" (Broussard 2018, p. 10), the kind of AI that is used in sci-fi movies with robots taking over the government and giving us a dark vision of the future of humans. But why should we create such a monster that aims to wipe us out completely someday?

The intention and wish of creating an *artificial general intelligence* have been inspirations for many science-fiction tales and movies and at the same time divide the community of researchers in the field. Researchers disagree on the forecast, when (or if) such an artificial general intelligence will be achieved, and whether it is even worth targeting this kind of artificial intelligence. Artificial general intelligence can also be defined as the "ability to accomplish any cognitive task at least as well as humans" (Tegmark 2018, p. 39).

Any cognitive task. That's quite complete. As Tegmark (2018) describes, based on such a general artificial intelligence, a *superintelligence* could be built, which can be used or unleased to take over the world. With superintelligence, he refers to "general intelligence far beyond human level" (Tegmark 2018, S. 39). This hypothetical moment in time, with unforeseen consequences for human civilization, is also referred to as *technology singularity*.

Certainly, there would still be a long way to go to reach something like this, at a technical level. Will we ever achieve something like this? Hard to predict. Does it make sense to aim at building this kind of a superintelligence (or a system with capabilities to potentially *break out* and create itself a superintelligence)? That's something we all should discuss, as a society.

Take a step back and consider the use cases where advanced technology could be beneficial as a tool to humans, as we are using other tools like calculators or cars. Now consider the scenario of creating a superintelligence, in form of armed robots or just by fully simulating being a human. One could be wondering, *why humans*? Would you be wanting to do that?

I encourage us as a society to think about what is useful for us in terms of technology, rather than developing technology that aims apocalyptic scenarios for mankind. Whereas there might be a fascination to be the creator of a *superintelligence*, it is not what the society or humanity needs.

Coming back to the language models. The way state-of-the-art language models or chatbot talk to us, simulating how humans would write, yet with major differences when it comes to meaning or communication intention, might be impressive. Still, they are a tool, a tool that provides us many opportunities and at the same time a tool that brings some risks along. The risks for the near future do not lay in the apocalyptic scenario of ChatGPT taking over the world but in other important discussions that need to be conducted now.

This split of the AI community was also visible in the case of *the letter* in spring 2023. As a consequence of the release of OpenAIs ChatGPT and in particular the GPT-4 model, the Future of Life Institute published an open letter signed by more than 10,000 supporters (Future of Life Institute 2023). Among the supporters, you can find professors from the field of AI, a Turing prize winner, and co-founders of well-known tech companies. In this letter, they call on all centers developing AI to pause for at least 6 months the training of AI systems more powerful than GPT-4. They argued that contemporary AI systems are becoming human-competitive at general tasks and that they should only be developed once we are confident that their effects will be positive and their risks manageable. The proposed pause of 6 months should be public and verifiable and, if necessary, enforced by governments applying a moratorium.

The letter was heavily discussed in the media. In addition to the need of a pause, in particular, the feasibility of the proposed a moratorium was put in question. The authors of the paper describing large language models as stochastic parrots (Bender et al. 2021), which we have encountered earlier, have shortly after published a statement regarding the letter (Gebru et al. 2023). In their statement, they discussed the need for regulatory efforts focusing on transparency, accountability, and prevention of exploitive labor practice, with a focus on AI that is already now real and present, deployed in automated systems. In particular, they criticized the fearmongering with hypothetical risks like "human-competitive intelligence" or "powerful digital minds." They argued that the letter ignores harms such as worker exploitation, massive data theft, synthetic media data reproducing systems of oppression and endangering the information ecosystem, and the concentration of power which exacerbates social inequities. Especially, they warned that:

> Such language that inflates the capabilities of automated systems and anthropomorphizes them, as we note in Stochastic Parrots, deceives people into thinking that there is a sentient being behind the synthetic media. This not only lures people into uncritically trusting the outputs of systems like ChatGPT, but also misattributes agency. Accountability properly lies not with the artifacts but with their builders. (Gebru et al. 2023)

Therefore, they underlined the need for regulation that enforces transparency and that regulations should protect the rights and interests of people when this technology is being applied by corporations.

Whether today's existing models like GPT-4 do have first signs of human-like intelligence or not is also influenced by the definition of intelligence itself.

Different definitions are being used and are discussed, and how to measure this intelligence is not finally decided. To sharpen the discussion, common definitions will need to be developed in the public discourse.

As we have seen throughout this book, language models can hallucinate and require additional e-literacy skills to be handled in a responsible manner. At the same time, people might interpret information provided by a chatbot differently from the information provided in a bullet list in the results of a search engine. There are risks when it comes to discrimination and bias in these systems, as well as expensive ecological consequences. Finally, the way machines and humans collaborate, in terms of work or learning, might change, requiring an adaptation of how we have been doing things so far. In a similar way, an adaptation was required when calculators were entering the market.

So, rather than worrying about the Terminator AI, let's look at the more pressing changes these new tools bring to our society and how to deal with them.

The Future of Responsible AI

From a technical perspective, the problems of hallucinations or bias in language models are difficult to address. Different technical methods exist to reduce hallucinations, either being applied to the data used for training or to the training process itself (Ji et al. 2023). In the training process, the components such as the encoder, the decoder, or the attention mechanism can be optimized to have a better semantic understanding of the input. For the data, the dataset can be increased or validated. One method that can be used is to create a (more) faithful dataset in collaboration with humans. As we have seen in different parts of this book, a language model can only be as good as the data it was trained on. Obtaining high-quality and faithful training data in the required quantity is challenging. One way to improve the training data is by employing human annotators. Human annotators can either write new texts from scratch or go through the training data and correcting or improving the collected texts.[1] In both cases, the required resources in terms of human labor, and thus costs, is very large. Therefore, this is often in the best case feasible for very domain-specific tasks and lacks generalization.

---

[1] Applying human annotations at a large scale and sometimes on sensitive topics such as discriminatory or offensive contents brings ethical considerations, as we have also discussed in this book.

For example, if we take the entire training set of a large language model, containing billions of words, it is not feasible to manually review all of this by humans. However, if we say that we are in particular interested in being sure that the system is all correct about strawberries, we could pick out from the training data all sentences containing the word *strawberry*. This would probably reduce the number of sentences to be reviewed by hand by a lot, and maybe it would become feasible.

At a technical level, the quality of the training data and transparency are two major enablers for responsible AI. Responsible AI, or in the context of this book *responsible natural language processing*, is a field that should interest us in order to shape the digital society we would like to have for the future. This raises also to the question of whether there is *the* digital society or whether there will be several digital societies involving different groups or regions.

To enable transparency about data sets, we first need a standard for documentation of datasets. Such a standard was proposed in the Datasheets for Datasets paper in 2021 (Gebru et al. 2021). The authors argue that the characteristics of the training data set influence the model's behavior, and thus the provenance, the creation, and the use of such data sets, need to be well documented. They suggest that each data set is accompanied by a data sheet, containing all this information. Sounds plausible and simple, but, unfortunately, it is currently not (yet) the default standard for the AI industry.

Apart from having more knowledge about the training data sets, we also want to be transparent about the machine learning models. And here it is getting a bit trickier. Whereas decisions obtained with the basic methods we have seen earlier in the beginning of the book, such as logistic regression, can be explained easier, when it comes to neural networks, this is very challenging. This problem is addressed by the research field of *explainable AI*. In the context of explainable AI, tools and frameworks are developed to understand and interpret the decisions such systems make. A better understanding of how decisions are made is required to be transparent about machine learning models. Unfortunately, more work is required in this field, and fully explaining how a 175 billion parameter language model generates a sentence is far from being solved.

Finally, as mentioned earlier, regulations of AI are another topic of the current discussion. Whereas most people agree that regulations are required, how they shall be implemented technically or enforced is subject to discussion. Whereas there might be few people being against fair and transparent AI software, it is challenging to fully address this at a technical level. However, we need this transparency and will thus need to rethink the way such software is developed and deployed. There is work ahead.

As we have seen now, the technical solution to these problems is still work in progress and, by design, difficult to fix. However, language models are used more and more, so we have to address some of these problems also at a societal level.

The Future of Work

New tools may change the way human work happens. To what extent should on one side be defined by what is technically possible but also by what is beneficial from a financial perspective and, most importantly, by what makes sense from a societal perspective. Personal computers and printers have revolutionized the technical way in which we write and produce text, shifting from handwritten notes to digital documents. With the introduction of smartphones, yet new ways of written communication such as SMS or messaging services have been introduced. With a new generation of tools like ChatGPT, text production by humans is challenged on a new level.

Whereas at a technical level it is now possible to produce texts that look somewhat eloquent and legit, they have major limitations in terms of content and world knowledge, as we have seen throughout this book. When with the rise of ChatGPT people suggested adding such a generative AI as coauthor to their scientific paper, it is them putting the technology in the job of a human. This is more a societal rather than a technical problem, and we should ask ourselves how we see our role and technology's role in all of this. If you use a generative AI to support you generating the structure of your scientific article, do you consider it your coauthor? Or let me rephrase it: Did you ever consider putting your text-processing tool like Word or Latex or the search engine you used to find related work as a coauthor?

How we define the power relationship between humans and machines for different tasks is crucial. Being a coauthor means seeing the tool at the same power level as your human coauthor. Having an AI application give severe instructions to human workers might reduce the acceptance of the technology as opposed to a human worker seeing a software as a smart tool supporting their working processes. For example, worker surveillance tools would probably be seen much more critical than an AI tool that is used as a programming assistant for software developers. To represent their processes in a useful and acceptable way in digital workflows and enable a human-centered digital transformation requires user involvement in all steps. This is especially true for novel technologies such as generative AI.

Additionally, with the stereotypes and limitations we have seen previously, I can only encourage having a *human in the loop*. As we have seen in the very early sections of this book, machine learning models, for example, classifiers, make an *estimation*. This guess, which seems the most probable for the given scenario, can also be *wrong*. Depending on what kind of critical decisions we are taking, we need to include more than the knowledge from the training data and reflect the proposed decisions by humans having world knowledge and experience. Additionally, as humans can be biased too, the processes and documentation around relevant decisions are crucial, also when being made by humans.

Are all AI applications critical in the same way? Probably not. When considering a software to sort different types of screws into boxes, there are probably much less ethical and human-in-the-loop problems as compared to other applications in the legal or medical domain. Systems that call for regulation and monitoring are those making decisions about "people, resources that concern people, issues that affect people's ability to participate in society" (Zweig 2022, p. 8).

With all that being said, I want to explain you why I do not like the term *artificial intelligence*. As mentioned, the goal of the society should be to produce tools supporting us with our tasks, and not aiming to develop a fully humanlike general artificial intelligence. The term *artificial intelligence*, even though established nowadays and widely used, is therefore misleading.

Therefore, the term *augmented intelligence*[2] is more and more used instead. It aims at the creation of technology that augments the human intelligence with smart tools, rather than replacing humans. This vision for the digital society of the future leaves the human in the control position and assesses the information provided by the software systems. As seen before, this is particularly relevant for critical use cases, such as decisions about humans.

As shown in Fig. 7.1, augmented intelligence aims to empower human decision-making, providing additional information and insights rather than replacing the human in the loop by a software.

The Future of Education

Let's now discuss what these technologies mean for education. Given the new possibilities of text generation with models like ChatGPT, several challenges arise for the way we were, until a few months ago quite successfully, teaching

---

[2] See, e.g., https://digitalreality.ieee.org/publications/what-is-augmented-intelligence.

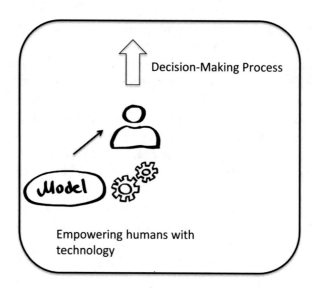

Fig. 7.1 Augmented intelligence: empowering humans rather than replacing them

and assessing students at different levels. By prompting ChatGPT (or other similar tools), it is now in many cases possible to solve programming exercises or write essays just by pasting the task description as a prompt. In other domains, it was reported that ChatGPT successfully passed exams that require domain-specific knowledge, as for example in medicine. What does this mean for our education system?

We have to review the way we teach and what the skills are that need to be developed by students but also for teachers or the broad public. The main challenge here is that technology is evolving fast, and to reflect the way we teach is taking more time. Rather than banning these tools, I suggest teaching our students how to use them responsibly and, in particular, what are their limitations and pitfalls.

We certainly have to adapt and review certain types of exams and some of the contents and skills we are aiming to teach and maybe have more direct interactions in the assessment rather than just an essay submitted at the end of the semester. But the new technologies offer much more than that. New generative AI tools also enable new great opportunities in the field of education, for example, to generate new use cases to discuss and critically reflect with students and to provide them with smart learning environments with individual feedback and suggestions. Human creativity along with the latest technology will shape the education of the future.

Apart impacting the way we work, learn, and teach, language models can provide also many interesting new questions for other fields of research, to be unfolded over the coming years. As the mathematician Stephen Wolfram is suggesting in his recent book about ChatGPT, "human language (and the patterns of thinking behind it) are somehow simpler and more *law like* in their structure than we thought" (Wolfram 2023, p. 108). Maybe those new technologies can finally help us in some way or the other to better understand ourselves.

Conclusion: Shaping the Future

We have seen in this book what is behind the scenes of state-of-the-art language models and in particular chatbots. Even though we have seen that from the inside language models are less magical than one might have thought in the beginning, their results are still impressive. By providing responses that might most likely look like good human answers to the proposed prompts, they give us the impression of eloquent conversation partners. These pitfalls and limitations need to be considered, yet there are nearly endless new opportunities that these technologies bring along for our society. It is what we make from it. And with *we*, I mean all of us. I want to encourage a public discourse about technology, involving technical experts as well as people from other domains. It is in our hands.

References

Ahn J, Oh A (2021) Mitigating Language-Dependent Ethnic Bias in BERT. In Proceedings of the 2021 Conference on Empirical Methods in Natural Language Processing (pp. 533-549).

Alammar J (2018) The Illustrated Transformer [Blog Post]. Available at https://jalammar.github.io/illustrated-transformer, last accessed 20.05.2023.

Bender EM, Gebru T, McMillan-Major A, Shmitchell S (2021) On the Dangers of Stochastic Parrots: Can Language Models Be Too Big?. In Proceedings of the 2021 ACM conference on fairness, accountability, and transparency (pp. 610-623).

Beuth P, Hoffmann H, Hoppenstedt M (2023) Die Gesichter hinter der KI. Der Spiegel Nr. 29.

Bolukbasi T, Chang KW, Zou JY, Saligrama V, Kalai AT (2016) Man is to computer programmer as woman is to homemaker? debiasing word embeddings. Advances in neural information processing systems, 29.

Broussard M (2018) Artificial unintelligence: How computers misunderstand the world. MIT Press.

Caliskan A, Bryson JJ, Narayanan A (2017) Semantics derived automatically from language corpora contain human-like biases. Science, 356(6334), 183-186.

Ciechanowski L, Przegalinska A, Magnuski M, Gloor P (2019) In the shades of the uncanny valley: An experimental study of human–chatbot interaction. Future Generation Computer Systems, 92, 539-548.

Coulter M, Bensinger G (2023) Alphabet shares dive after Google AI chatbot Bard flubs answer in ad. Reuters. Available at https://www.reuters.com/technology/google-ai-chatbot-bard-offers-inaccurate-information-company-ad-2023-02-08/, last accessed 27.05.2023.

© The Author(s), under exclusive license to Springer Nature Switzerland AG 2023
M. Kurpicz-Briki, *More than a Chatbot*, https://doi.org/10.1007/978-3-031-37690-0

Crawford K (2021) Atlas of AI: Power, Politics, and the Planetary Costs of Artificial Intelligence. Yale University Press.

Devlin J, Chang MW, Lee K, Toutanova K (2019) BERT: Pre-training of Deep Bidirectional Transformers for Language Understanding. In Proceedings of the 2019 Conference of the North American Chapter of the Association for Computational Linguistics: Human Language Technologies, Volume 1 (Long and Short Papers) (pp. 4171-4186).

Dräger J, Müller-Eiselt R (2020) We Humans and the Intelligent Machines: How algorithms shape our lives and how we can make good use of them. Verlag Bertelsmann Stiftung.

Eubanks V (2018) *Automating inequality: How high-tech tools profile, police, and punish the poor.* St. Martin's Press.

Firth JR (1962) A synopsis of linguistic theory, 1930-1955. Studies in linguistic analysis, Oxford.

Future of Life Institute (2023) Pause Giant AI Experiments: An Open Letter. Available at https://futureoflife.org/open-letter/pause-giant-ai-experiments, last accessed 21.05.2023.

Gebru T, Morgenstern J, Vecchione B, Vaughan JW, Wallach H, Iii HD, Crawford K (2021) Datasheets for datasets. Communications of the ACM, 64(12), 86-92.

Gebru T, Bender EM, McMillan-Major A, Mitchell M (2023) Statement from the Listed Authors of Stochastic Parrots on the "AI Pause" Letter. Available at https://www.dair-institute.org/blog/letter-statement-March2023, last accessed 21.05.2023.

Grave É, Bojanowski P, Gupta P, Joulin A, Mikolov T (2018) Learning Word Vectors for 157 Languages. In Proceedings of the Eleventh International Conference on Language Resources and Evaluation (LREC 2018).

Hagiwara M (2021) Real-world natural language processing. Manning Publishing.

Hancox P (1996) A brief history of natural language processing. Available at https://www.cs.bham.ac.uk/~pjh/sem1a5/pt1/pt1_history.html, last accessed 27.05.2023.

Honert M (2017) People vs. robots. "Evolution doesn't care whether we are happy.". Goethe Institut. Available at https://www.goethe.de/ins/ca/en/kul/met/phm/21367294.html, last accessed 27.05.2023.

Ji Z, Lee N, Frieske R, Yu T, Su D, Xu Y, Ishii E, Bang Y, Dai W, Madotto A, Fung P (2023) Survey of hallucination in natural language generation. ACM Computing Surveys, 55(12), 1-38.

Joshi P, Santy S, Budhiraja A, Bali K, Choudhury M (2020) The State and Fate of Linguistic Diversity and Inclusion in the NLP World. In Proceedings of the 58th Annual Meeting of the Association for Computational Linguistics (pp. 6282-6293).

Jurafsky D, Martin JH (2023) Speech and Language Processing: An Introduction to Natural Language Processing, Computational Linguistics, and Speech Recognition. Draft 3rd Edition.

Lane H, Howard C, Hapke HM (2019) Natural language processing in action. Understanding, analyzing und generating text with Python. Manning Publishing.

Mikolov T, Sutskever I, Chen K, Corrado GS, Dean, J (2013) Distributed representations of words and phrases and their compositionality. Advances in neural information processing systems, 26.

Mikolov T, Grave É, Bojanowski P, Puhrsch C, Joulin A. (2018) Advances in Pre-Training Distributed Word Representations. In Proceedings of the Eleventh International Conference on Language Resources and Evaluation (LREC 2018).

Mori M (1970) The uncanny valley: the original essay by Masahiro Mori. IEEE Spectrum.

Nida-Rümelin, J, & Weidenfeld, N (2022) *Digital Humanism: For a Humane Transformation of Democracy, Economy and Culture in the Digital Age.* Springer Nature.

Pennington J, Socher R, Manning CD (2014) Glove: Global vectors for word representation. In Proceedings of the 2014 conference on empirical methods in natural language processing (EMNLP) (pp. 1532-1543).

Perrigo B (2023) Exclusive: OpenAI Used Kenyan Workers on Less Than $2 Per Hour to Make ChatGPT Less Toxic. The TIME. Available at https://time.com/6247678/openai-chatgpt-kenya-workers/, last accessed 23.05.2023.

Plecháč P (2021) Relative contributions of Shakespeare and Fletcher in Henry VIII: An analysis based on most frequent words and most frequent rhythmic patterns. Digital Scholarship in the Humanities, 36(2), 430-438.

Rashid T (2017) Neuronale Netze selbst programmieren: ein verständlicher Einstieg mit Python. O'Reilly. Originally in English: Rashid, T. (2016). Make your own neural network. CreateSpace Independent Publishing Platform.

Shah C, Bender EM (2022). Situating search. In ACM SIGIR Conference on Human Information Interaction and Retrieval (pp. 221-232).

Søraa RA (2023) *AI for Diversity*. CRC Press.

Strubell E, Ganesh A, McCallum A (2019) Energy and Policy Considerations for Deep Learning in NLP. In Proceedings of the 57th Annual Meeting of the Association for Computational Linguistics (pp. 3645-3650).

Tegmark M (2018) Life 3.0: Being human in the age of artificial intelligence. Penguin Books.

Turing AM (1950) Computing machinery and intelligence. Mind, 59, 433–460.

Vaswani A, Shazeer N, Parmar N, Uszkoreit J, Jones L, Gomez AN, Kaiser L, Polosukhin I (2017) Attention is all you need. Advances in neural information processing systems, 30.

Vosoughi S, Roy D, Aral S (2018) The spread of true and false news online. science, 359(6380), 1146-1151.

Weizenbaum J (1966) ELIZA—a computer program for the study of natural language communication between man and machine. Communications of the ACM, 9(1), 36-45.

Windhager S, Slice DE, Schaefer K, Oberzaucher E, Thorstensen T, Grammer K (2008) Face to face: The perception of automotive designs. Human Nature, 19, 331-346.

Wolfram S (2023) What Is ChatGPT Doing ... and Why Does It Work? Wolfram Media, Inc.

Zweig KA (2022) Awkward Intelligence: Where AI Goes Wrong, why it Matters, and what We Can Do about it. MIT Press.